The Authors

Maralene and Miles Wesner are multi-talented teachers and prolific writers. They have published more than 150 Audio-Visual Education aids, and pioneered new reading methods with their Phonics in a Nutshell (1965).

They have written articles, and mission studies for Southern Baptist periodicals. They were in the original group of writers to develop WMU's Big "A" Club material.

They've published several books with Broadman Press: *A Fresh Look at the Gospel* (1983); *You Are What You Choose* (1984); and *How To Be a Saint When You Feel Like a Sinner* (1986) and self-published 30 books by Diversity Press.

They are noted for their no-nonsense style, their clear illustrations, and their willingness to face controversial issues. From the dual perspectives of both academic and religious professions, they seek to be a bridge between the spiritual and the intellectual worlds.

They hold Masters Degrees (MEd) from Oklahoma University plus work toward a Doctorate. Miles also attended Southwestern Baptist Theological Seminary, and served as a high school counselor. He has been the bi-vocational pastor of a small rural church for more than 50 years.

Both Maralene and Miles taught in public school and collages and served as educational consultants. Maralene taught Psychology and Speech for Southeastern Oklahoma State University for 32 years. She was chosen Oklahoma Teacher of the Year in 1975.

They have planned, led tours, and done research in all of the 50 states, Canada, Mexico, Europe, Egypt, Japan, and the Holy Land. In 1985, they were among a small group of Americans who were invited by Dr. Joseph P. Kennedy of the US/China Education Foundation and Bishop Ting, leader of the Three Self Movement, to participate in the First Symposium on the Church in Nanjing, China.

Now, they use their lifetime of varied experiences to write insightful sermons, essays, and books.

Titles by Maralene & Miles Wesner
published by Nurturing Faith

Sermons for Special Days

Life More Abundant

Do You Really Know Jesus?

If Jesus Were Here Today

101 Sparks of Inspiration

When God Can't Answer

Think (Or Else!)

Stumbling TO ZION

Today's Church in Today's World

Maralene & Miles Wesner

© 2022
Published in the United States by Nurturing Faith, Macon, GA.
Nurturing Faith is a book imprint of Good Faith Media (goodfaithmedia.org).
Library of Congress Cataloging-in-Publication Data is available.

ISBN: 978-1-63528-210-8

All rights reserved. Printed in the United States of America.

Scripture quotations are from New Revised Standard Version Bible Updated Edition, copyright © 2021 National Council of the Churches of Christ in the United States of America. Used by permission. All rights reserved worldwide.

Cover photograph by David Cassady.

Contents

Rationale 1
I. The Background of the Church 3
II. The Theology of the Church 21
III. The Practices of the Church.. 37
IV. The Role of the Church 53
V. The Leadership of the Church 71
VI. The Challenge of the Church 89

Rationale

We've pastored churches for more than fifty years and taught in public schools and universities for many years. We've also published both religious and educational materials. Our whole life has been dedicated to bridging the gap between the spiritual and the intellectual worlds. Therefore, when we were asked to develop and teach a course in religion for a state college, we viewed it as an exciting challenge.

We believe faith must be practical and religion must be relevant. With these principles in mind, we wrote a course that surveys today's church. It's not our purpose to compare religions or prove doctrine. Instead, this book examines the "other side." It avoids the orthodox party line. It seeks to disturb complacency, override conditioning, and challenge mindset. It moves parables out of the first century and presents new spiritual models.

We encourage readers to analyze and actualize their faith. Some observations may be provoking and disturbing, but any criticism comes from concern rather than from cynicism.

Whether you are religious or not—whether your views are liberal, conservative, or fundamental—we believe you will profit from information concerning these vital issues. It's our objective to eliminate spiritual illiteracy and enable individuals to speak intelligently when doctrinal and ethical questions arise.

We hope this book will help both leaders and churches to begin truly marching—instead of stumbling—to Zion!

I
The Background of the Church

Jesus said, "I will build my church, and the gates of Hades will not prevail against it" (Matt 16:18). When he realized his time on earth was coming to an end, Jesus began considering how he could make his valuable insights and teachings available to future generations. He also realized this wouldn't be easy. People are averse to change, especially to any change in religious beliefs.

Over and over in the Gospels, we hear Jesus's adversaries inquiring, "By what authority do you do these things?" Even today, if we advocate new ideas, we still hear cynics asking, "By what authority do you speak?" They usually mean, "What expert are you quoting? What tradition are you following? What legal opinion are you citing?"

Unfortunately, operating on the basis of some accepted authority can be a hollow criterion for evaluation. Indeed, it can be downright dangerous. Authorities are notorious for being wrong! For many centuries all the accepted scientific authorities taught that the earth was flat. For many centuries all the accepted political authorities taught that a monarchy was the only viable form of government. For many centuries all the accepted medical authorities taught that bleeding cured illnesses. Experts told Beethoven he was hopeless. They told Thomas Edison he was too stupid to learn in school.

It's obvious that statements should not be evaluated on the basis of who said them. They should be evaluated on the basis of their own validity. We must judge things by their results. Jesus said, "You will know them by their fruits" (Matt 7:20).

It's axiomatic that no one has any authority to promote that which is false, and no one needs any authority to promote that which is true. Jesus said, "Wisdom is vindicated by all her children" (Luke 7:35). He meant that the truth of an idea is proved by its effects and the results it produces, not by who said it.

Nevertheless, most individuals and institutions do depend upon some base of authority. Traditional authority is not as helpful as it once was because civilization is changing much faster than ever before. What the past generation did is usually too remote and irrelevant to be effective in this generation.

For instance, a farmer, teaching his son how to harness a mule, how to hold a plow, and how to distribute fertilizer by hand is giving useless information to modern agriculturalists with complex mechanical equipment and new chemical additives.

A woman teaching her daughter how to start a fire in a wood stove and how to test for temperature with water drops wastes her time if the daughter has a modern range and a microwave oven.

Some overall life principles—such as determination, discipline, and good management skills—remain valid, but specific details are quickly becoming obsolete. The same is true with doctrines and ethics. Some overall principles remain valid, but specific details are worthless.

Scriptural authority is also hindered because the Bible developed out of a different time, a different culture, and a different language. Words and their meanings vary drastically. New issues arise, and circumstances change. With every passing year biblical language and subject matter seems to speak less and less specifically to our own concerns.

Twenty-first-century humanity is moving away from a world of rulers and masters. As we become more educated and liberated, there is less and less emphasis on absolute obedience to external regulations. In all other areas of life, we are becoming more democratic, autonomous, and self-directive. Any doctrine, therefore, that discourages personal maturity and responsibility is destined to become obsolete. A man living in 1900 was closer to Abraham in lifestyle than he was to us! Furthermore, in a rapidly progressing civilization, absolute scriptural authority holds us to the past. When we bump a "biblical stump," we are forced to stand there and mark time while the world marches on.

Well-meaning Christians once used scriptures to prove that the earth was flat. After all, it has "four corners" (see Ezek 7:2). They argued that slavery is ordained of God because Paul admonished slaves to obey their masters (see Eph 6:5). They maintained that the sun goes around the earth because Joshua prayed for it to stop (see Josh 10:12–13). Christianity even opposed the discovery of anesthesia because it was used to alleviate the pain of childbirth. They said women were "supposed to be punished by God for Eve's rebellion" (see Gen 3:16).

Furthermore, churches often become preoccupied with a few theological dogmas mentioned in the scriptures and ignore the numerous current issues that aren't. The Bible talks about swords, which we don't use, but it doesn't talk about automatic rifles, which we do use! Also, religious leaders have always tended to rely more on the external authorities, such as tradition and scripture, than they have on the internal authority of the Holy Spirit.

Over the years blind obedience has been greatly overrated as a virtue. The only viable alternative to external authority is personal authority, but this risky stance has only been encouraged by a handful of individual mavericks from Jeremiah to Jesus. Sometimes in the final analysis personal authority has dared to pit "one man against the world." The personal authority base has obvious strengths. It is willing to put human reason, experience, and autonomy above all else.

Ever since the age of enlightenment, the scientific method of thought has permeated the whole world. We use personal authority in economics, politics, and education. Inductive processes of discovery and discernment encourage individual autonomy. Moreover, maintaining a democracy in a complex and changing society requires internal decision-making.

Nevertheless, the limitations of this base are obvious. It can literally promote an "every man for himself" mentality. This can lead to chaos. It can destabilize society. There is always great danger involved when large numbers of immature individuals try to operate without any externally imposed guidelines. It can be like turning children loose with dynamite.

In spite of the hazards, however, it's still the most viable system. Indeed, since it's open-ended and adaptable, it seems to be the only system that can survive and meet the future needs of society. Intelligent, responsible, caring people can and must learn to handle such liberty.

The personal authority base was given credence at Pentecost. This experience didn't repudiate or replace the traditions and the scriptures, but it did give the Holy Spirit credence and allowed it to operate. Jesus said, "The Holy Spirit, whom the Father will send in my name, will teach you everything and remind you of all that I have said to you" (John 14:26). The personal authority base increased the number of new perspectives. It emphasized "living water" and gave freedom to the God within.

It's obvious that modern Christians cannot depend upon any one absolute, external authority base. No matter how devoutly you believe the Bible, it won't tell you how to vote on the use of military drones, whether to attempt an infertility procedure to have a baby, or if it's moral to accept a kidney transplant. Instead, we must consider and integrate truth from all sources. Our inner urges include both conscience and reason. Scriptural and religious tradition includes revelation and historical experience. Practical considerations include real life circumstances and personal opportunities. These three, taken together, can provide a realistic guide for making productive decisions.

It's obvious that Christian teachings and doctrines cannot be understood without some background information. A survey of Old Testament history from the progressive revelation perspective will note those customs, taboos, and events that later influenced the gospel and the church. Without understanding the cultural context, many traditional practices and scriptural passages can easily become superstitions.

A recent newspaper reported that hospital officials had gone to court to argue for the continuation of blood transfusions for a sick child. The doctors said that in this case, without a blood transfusion, the disease would be fatal. The parents had objected because of religious beliefs and quoted a scripture that says, "Abstain…from blood" (Acts 15:29).

You see, many beliefs can become hindrances. God and his truth don't change, but our perceptions of them do. As tourists in South Dakota, we may strain for a glimpse of the famous Mt. Rushmore. At first we see it faintly, far away, dimmed by early morning fog and partly obstructed by the hills and trees. As we approach the area, however, it becomes clearer and clearer. The fog lifts. The trees are left behind. Finally, as we come around a mountain, there it is in all its magnificence—distinct and beautiful! Now, Mt. Rushmore didn't change. We did! Our position, our perspective, and our perception made all the difference.

Discernment of God's progressive revelation helps bridge the gap between antiquity and the twenty-first century. The strange phenomenon of a God who "walks in the garden," a God who "speaks aloud" to eight-hundred-year-old patriarchs, and a God who zaps fantastic miracles creates a vast gulf between modern Christians and the scriptures. Since we obviously don't experience such marvels, we conclude that either the natural principles in those early times, or even God himself, were somehow different. Furthermore, if we can't identify with them, then we can't learn from them.

Also, ethical conflicts can present insurmountable barriers. Trying to "explain" certain questionable and offensive statements concerning divine attitudes and deeds requires incredible mental gymnastics. Indeed, many moral, rational individuals are forced to conclude that this wrathful creature depicted in the Old Testament wasn't the God of love whom Jesus called "Abba, Father." Such incongruous, untenable conflicts must be reconciled.

Some of these distortions can be eliminated if we realize the limitations of early thought. The belief system of primitive people included several basic assumptions. These almost universal outlooks colored their view of life and their interpretation of history. Our teachings, our experiences, and our conditioning color and influence our view of life. We can't escape our culture and our heritage.

The first assumption they had was that God did everything personally. He instigated or supervised every single event. They knew of no other power source. They had no information about neutral processes or natural laws. Therefore, every time a leaf fell, they saw it as a distinct divine act. They believed God's moment-to-moment whims caused such things as deaths, accidents, floods, storms, and earthquakes. Because of this simplistic outlook, atrocious deeds were often attributed to God. Some of the oldest writings tell us that God, in fits of anger, destroyed people, cities, nations, and indeed almost the whole world. This is an unfair and demeaning description of our heavenly Father.

The second assumption was that since God is both powerful and whimsical, it behooved people to keep him in a good mood. They tried to do this through various spiritual bribes. Sacrifices, rituals, vows, promises, offerings, and worship practices were developed in pathetic attempts to placate a terrifying supernatural being. Even the word *holy* is sometimes associated with fear and punishment (see Num 4:15–20).

Their self-preservation methods and submissive pleas were based on the idea that God could repent or be persuaded to change his mind (see Exod 32:14). This less-than-divine attribute is insinuated in many episodes. After all, if we can't persuade him, then why should we pray or worship? That's an immature concept. A God who can be influenced by our childish whims and notions would destroy the universe. We need a consistent, dependable, immutable God.

Nevertheless, even today, almost everybody bargains with God. In emergencies we say, "Oh, God, if you'll only do this for me, I'll do this, this, and this!" We're like the two fellows lost at sea: One kneels in the raft and prays, "Please, Lord, save us, and we'll go to church, tithe, quit gambling." The other yells, "Hey, wait a minute. Don't promise anything else. I think I see a ship."

Such bargaining is understandable but immature. We don't realize its implications. Omnipotence without omniscience would be a curse! Absolute power without absolute wisdom and absolute love would be deadly!

Suppose you had the ability to bargain with God. What would you be willing to sacrifice to win the lottery, close that great business deal, or satisfy some deep desire? If your child was in an accident, wouldn't you trade another young person's life to save his? If you had a terminal illness, wouldn't you annihilate faceless people in Afghanistan to get well? All of us would! We're human beings. We're selfish by nature. We have a survival instinct that overrides altruism. We'd wreck the universe to get our own way.

Furthermore, such omnipotence would put us in a "catch 22" position: If we could save our loved ones by making a deal with God and didn't, we'd die of guilt. But if we could save our loved ones and did make a deal that harmed someone else, we'd also die of guilt. That's why we can't be omnipotent until we are also omniscient, with full knowledge of consequences. We can't bargain with God until we're totally spiritual beings without earthly egos. Bargaining sounds good, but it entails awesome responsibilities that we are not equipped to handle.

After the idea of a dual system of both good and evil was developed, then God was seen as the ultimate benevolent creator and Satan as the rebellious adversary. Along with these opposite forces came a hierarchy of lesser gods. The good ones were presented as angels, messengers, and holy spirits. The bad ones were viewed as devils, demons, and evil spirits. Everything from mental illness to communicable diseases were thought to be caused by such demons.

Since primitive people had no knowledge of biological or psychological principles, they attributed physical phenomena such as shivers, chill bumps, sneezes, fevers, seizures, and heart palpitations to spells cast by demons. A person suffering with any anomaly or handicap was, therefore, thought to be under the control of Satan.

That's why eccentric old ladies were burned as witches. That's why epileptic children were beaten to death. That's why painful exorcisms were carried out on the mentally deranged. That's why those who were crippled or mutilated were excluded from temple worship.

After good and evil were perceived, a crude moral system was devised. Simply put, this code insisted that the scales must balance! From this assumption came the slogan "An eye for an eye, a tooth for a tooth"—a payment for a transgression.

The idea of remission by blood was part of this early development. Blood was seen as the essence of life. Indeed, it almost had a life of its own, as suggested when "Abel's blood cried out from the ground" for vengeance (see Gen 4:10). If blood epitomized life, then it and it alone could "atone" or pay for serious sins. At first the scales were made to balance by the actual sacrifice of human beings. This literally provided a life for a life.

When they threw children into volcanoes or sacrificed virgins on the altar, they were saying, "God, we'll give you this life if you'll spare ours." Later, animal substitutes were allowed. One scripture says, "The LORD said to Moses…'You need make for me only an altar of earth and sacrifice on it your burnt offerings and your offerings of well-being, your sheep and your oxen; in every place where I cause my name to be remembered I will come to you and bless you'" (Exod 20:22, 24).

Jeremiah, however, moved beyond this concept. He repudiated this earlier commandment, quoting God as saying, "In the day that I brought your ancestors out of the land of Egypt, I did not speak to them or command them concerning burnt offerings and sacrifices. But this command I gave them, 'Obey my voice, and I will be your God, and you shall be my people'" (Jer 7:22–23). This scripture explains that God didn't desire sacrifices. Instead, he simply allowed his immature followers to perform these acts to relieve their guilt.

The "balanced scale" moral system was also used to explain natural phenomena and historical events. People realized that catastrophes such as tornadoes, earthquakes, and military defeats had to have causes. Since they knew nothing of scientific or social processes, they assumed misfortunes must have moral causes. They had no idea that hot and cold air masses caused turbulence and storms, so it was natural for them to personalize the cause. Their first instinct was to ask, "What did I do to cause this tragedy?" When disaster struck, it was usually easy to find enough sins and shortcomings to justify the punishment received.

Unfortunately, however, things aren't consistent. We can say, "God destroyed Sodom and Gomorrah because they were seedbeds of wickedness," but we can't attribute the destruction of cities today to such causes. In a raging wildfire or a destructive hurricane, it's obvious that both brothels and churches are destroyed. Both criminals and innocent babies are killed.

All these primitive beliefs and uninformed assumptions must be taken into consideration when we read the Bible. Taboos and false conclusions result when two unrelated events are linked as cause and effect. That's how superstitions concerning Friday the thirteenth and broken mirrors originated. The customs of some native tribes prohibit certain kinds of work during holy weeks. The story is told of a woman who disregarded this taboo and went to the river to do her family's laundry. She never came back. When her family looked for her, all they found was the laundry on the bank and a big fish swimming in the river. They concluded, therefore, that she had been turned into a fish as punishment for her misdeed. Now, something did happen. A woman disappeared, and a fish was observed. Presto! These were linked together and formed a wholly unsubstantiated superstition.

In short, early scriptures show that individuals, in trying to understand the world around them, are also envisioning a god in their own image. Since good people tend to see a good god and evil people imagine an evil god, a group's level of maturity can often be judged by their concept of God.

Jesus remedied this to some degree. He said, "Whoever has seen me has seen the Father." If Jesus wouldn't behave in a certain way, then God wouldn't behave that way (see John 14:8–9). Such was the significance of his incarnation. Since we have a living personification of the divine creator, misconceptions can be minimized.

What kind of God do we have? Is he a vindictive dispenser of justice? An impersonal balancer of the moral scales? A loving and forgiving heavenly Father?

We may not fashion gods of clay or stone, but our concept of a god is fashioned just as surely in our imagination. We make him just as surely as the native fashions an idol of clay! We make him just as surely as the heathen carves an idol of stone. The god we are conditioned to believe in may be invisible, but that doesn't make them spiritual. If the nature, methods, morals, and actions of our object of worship are less than divine, that's an idol!

This issue concerning our concept of God is crucial because we will inevitably become like him. Ours must be the God was reflected in the life of our Lord and Savior Jesus Christ.

The problem of evil presents another age-old dilemma. A minister saw a weeping woman and described his possible responses this way: "I might have said, 'Lady, suffering is caused by sin. You haven't been living right, and now God is punishing you. You must repent!' But that's not always the right answer. I might have said, 'Your suffering is just in your mind. Things aren't as bad as they seem. Think positive thoughts!' But that's not always the right answer. I might have said, 'Suffering is good for you. Just as rough weather toughens the roots of the oak tree, so can your troubles strengthen your soul!' But that's not always the right answer."

What *is* the right answer?

The Old Testament prophets dealt with this question. They were the defenders of personal integrity. They were the passionately honest realists who even dared to argue with God. They addressed the issues that didn't fit traditional theology.

Remember, the scales must balance. If something bad happened, it had to be punishment for evil done; therefore, when parasites ate the crops and the vines dropped unripe fruit, it was interpreted as a sign of God's anger. Sometimes, however, there didn't seem to be any specific reason for it. Even when they paid their tithes and observed all the sacrifices, misery continued.

To make matters worse, they sometimes saw the obvious good fortune of those who openly ridiculed religion and defied the laws. This seemed blatantly unfair. The old formula of sin and punishment, righteousness and reward was absolutely inconsistent with reality. Sometimes there seemed to be no correlation between high quality of character and positive circumstances. One prophet complained, "All who do evil are good in the sight of the LORD.... Where is the God of justice?" (Mal 2:17).

Generations came and went, and justice was obviously not being meted out. In Jewish thinking the scales have to balance somewhere, so the hope of a resurrection and the idea of immortality emerged. There must be life after death, where the scales can finally be balanced.

These mavericks who questioned religion weren't popular. Opponents burned their books, but they couldn't destroy their insights (see Jer 36:27–32). The prophets lost every battle, but they won the war! Singlehandedly, they kept the idea of God from being identified with injustice. By picturing God as a righteous judge, they lifted the Hebrew religion above all others.

The scriptures concerning Job also deal with this question: "Why do the righteous suffer and the wicked prosper?" Those prophets considered the problem of good and evil and wrestled with the paradox of undeserved human tragedy. In other words, when we say, "Why me?" we're voicing Job's question.

The book of Job is a criticism of the Wisdom literature, which used the promise of earthly returns as an incentive to morality. The character Job exemplifies the very things that are supposed to ensure prosperity, yet terrible things happened to him! Advisors presented the orthodox platitudes, but platitudes did not prove sufficient. Rules may provide satisfactory guidelines for ordinary life, but the real heartbreaking experiences need other explanations.

The author could not accept the ancient belief that disaster is always chastisement from God, so he dramatized the fact that man's conduct and his earthly fate are not absolutely correlated. God is not simply a dispenser of material rewards and punishments. Those who believed God caused every event thought suffering had to be retribution. Even in the garden of Eden, physical labor and painful childbearing were interpreted as penalties for sin.

When anyone suffered adversity, others saw this as a sign of God's disfavor. Therefore, instead of respect, help, and sympathy, the unfortunate person was subjected to ridicule and mockery because everyone believed he must have done something wicked to bring this upon himself. This shows the negative results of a doctrine that encourages fortunate ones to feel "holier than thou" and thus justified in their condemnation of unfortunate victims.

Job's friends repeated all the old religious cliches because they thought they were indispensable to sound faith. When Job denied them, they said, "You're destroying religion!" (see Job 15:4). Even today, every innovator who opens new doors or asks new questions is so charged.

Job triumphed when he insisted that facts must take precedence over dogma! Job had watched good men destroyed and evil men spared. The refusal of his friends to face reality roused his indignation. He had eyes, and he saw! They had eyes too but saw nothing because they didn't want their comfortable faith questioned.

Throughout the ordeal Job kept his integrity. He didn't challenge the assumption that calamity ought to be punishment for sin, but he insisted that in his case it was not. Then with eyes sharpened by tragedy, Job looked around at other cases and concluded that the old formula was invalid. Things aren't always fair in this world. As one cynic asked, "Why does God take the good people to heaven and leave the bad ones here on earth to aggravate us?"

Even though Job found no meaningful answer, he believed there was one. He envisioned a future based on order and purpose, not chaos. That is true faith. God showed Job the bigger picture. Each of us must learn that there's more to this world than just me. There are complex processes. You can't fix one thing without messing up something else.

We must realize that nature and God are not synonymous. Nature is a neutral system. Nature includes the raw materials, the resources, and the processes of God, but these things have been put at our disposal. We're to "take dominion" over them, using and shaping them to constructive purposes. For example, diseases are for curing. Accidents are for preventing. Storms are for avoiding.

The healing process is just such a neutral system. God doesn't wave magic wands. Instead, he programmed wonderful cell regeneration possibilities into our natural equipment so that if we provide the right conditions, it occurs.

This neutral system is evident everywhere. For instance, why would God need to build in such redundancy if he personally supervises everything? Consider the conception/birth process. Men produce billions of sperm when only one is needed to fertilize the egg. Now, if God himself connected the sperm and the egg cells on a case-by-case basis, he wouldn't need great numbers to increase the odds. Instead, he created a self-perpetuating system that we must learn to use—not just passively accept. The fact that it's a neutral system explains why good people are sometimes infertile and child abusers have a house full of kids.

Before we decry the system, let's realize that life has two sides. To destroy one is to destroy the other. Good has bad. Love has hate. Truth has falsehood. You can't have one without the other.

There is a legend about a woman who came to the River Styx to be carried across to the next life. The man who ran the ferry reminded her she could drink of the sacred waters and thus forget the life she was leaving. Eagerly, she said, "You mean I will forget how I have suffered."

"Yes," he responded, "but you will also forget how you have rejoiced."

"I will forget my failures?" she asked.

"Yes, but you will also forget your successes."

"I will forget how I have been hated?" she said.

"Yes, but you will also forget how you have been loved."

The story ends with the woman deciding it is better to retain her memory of the good and the bad.

Life is always two-sided, and to destroy one side necessarily destroys the other. Again and again, we ask, "Why has this happened to me? Why sickness? Why handicaps? Why death? Pain in our bodies, pain in our minds, pain in our hearts—why does it have to be this way?" We can better understand the pain of life if we keep in mind several facts.

> 1. Every possible blessing is also a possible pain. For instance, suppose you bought a skateboard for your children. This could bring them great joy. However, using it also increases the possibility of injuries. Therefore, if your children fall on the concrete and have a concussion, would you say, "I caused their pain"? Well, in a sense you did, but by giving them the skateboard you also increased their possibilities for pleasure. By giving them the skateboard you were allowing them to get hurt, but that certainly was not your intent. The situation would have been different if you had deliberately banged their heads against the concrete.
>
> 2. God has provided wonderful things for our joy. Consider love, for example. Love brings life's greatest blessings, but it also brings life's greatest pains.
>
> 3. God gives us the capacity to dream. Sometimes we don't realize our dreams, and this brings disappointment and frustration. Sometimes, on the other hand,

we do realize our dreams and thus are able to know the thrill of achievement.

4. When a team plays a baseball game and is beaten, the defeat is hard to bear. They could have avoided their defeat by not playing the game, but, of course, they would also have denied themselves the chance to win. If we play the game, then we must accept the possibilities of winning and of losing.

Life's possibilities seem to come in pairs: good and evil, strong and weak, pleasure and pain. The existence of one carries with it the possibility of the other.

Pain in this life is one of the prices we must pay for belonging to the human family. If we insist that God set up the world on an individual basis, allowing each one to suffer merely to the extent of his own wrongdoing, then we must restrict all our joys to those we can bring upon ourselves. We enjoy a multitude of blessings we do not earn, and in the same way we suffer many pains we do not deserve.

Sometimes when tragedies occur, people say, "What have I done to cause this?" Often the answer is, "Nothing!" But neither have they done anything to earn many of their blessings. It's all part of belonging to the human family. Suffering is part of life, and we have to endure it. One little girl expressed it well. When she fell down and skinned her knee, she complained, "I wish the whole world was cushioned."

So what do we do when trouble comes? As Christians we are not supposed to accept misfortunes. We're to use them. Paul's imprisonment was not God's will. It represented the cruelty of man. Paul might have cursed his fate, raged against his jailers, and become bitter and rebellious. Or he might have meekly surrendered without complaint. In fact, he did neither. Instead, he used his misfortunes and turned that prison into a mission field.

There are many examples of people turning curses into blessings. In fact, everything that happens to us can be a potential gift, even our wounds, our disappointments, and our failures. The recovered alcoholic has the gift of speaking to other alcoholics in a way that a nonalcoholic cannot. The woman who has suffered a nervous breakdown has the gift of knowing what total mental collapse feels like and can listen sympathetically to others under stress. The man for whom gambling is a persistent problem can minister to others in a way that those who have no problems cannot. All these people have particular gifts that those individuals who have never been tested or stretched do not have.

Even bad situations and hurtful accidents can be transformed into gifts. One sports development is such an example: When they first manufactured golf balls, the surfaces were smooth. One young man who had severe financial difficulties loved to play golf. But he had only one beat-up golf ball, while the men he was playing with had new, smooth, shiny golf balls. Strangely enough, as they played, the poor kid's ball got a lot more distance and went straighter than the smooth balls. Today, all golf balls are manufactured with dimples. These rough spots cause the ball to go farther. So it is with life. It takes some rough spots to motivate us to greatness.

So what can Christians do about evil, about senseless tragedies, and about frustrating problems? Well, we must realize that this is an imperfect world and that it's our job to make it more perfect. Also, we must realize that to have pleasure, we must have the possibility of pain. Above all, we must realize that when the inevitable hurts and setbacks occur, we can salvage something from these experiences. We can learn from them. We can use them in positive ways. We can turn curses into blessings.

It's fortunate that over the years there were a few deep thinkers who challenged the status quo. It's fortunate that these courageous prophets refused to accept the belief that evil was ordained of God. These oddballs and mavericks were the forerunners of the church. They dealt with real problems and gave Christianity its credibility.

Even so, the church must not claim absolute traditional authority or absolute scriptural authority about every issue. Jesus promised that the Holy Spirit will live in each Christian. This divine power gives us the right to depend on our own internal, personal authority.

Jesus transferred tremendous authority to individuals. He believed men and women can be empowered by the Holy Spirit to think and decide and act for themselves. He said, "When the Spirit of truth comes, he will guide you into all the truth" (John 16:13).

Paul also affirmed this personal authority base, saying, "Each one of us will be held accountable" (Rom 14:12).

II

The Theology of the Church

Theological arguments and debates are common. Most people become disturbed when they realize there are other individuals and other groups who hold different beliefs. Religion causes many of the conflicts and disagreements that lead to criticism, hostility, and violence.

The disciples of John came to Jesus, saying, "Why do we and the Pharisees fast often, but your disciples do not fast?" He explained that the attendants of a bridegroom don't grieve while the bridegroom is with them. Then he gave an interesting analogy about changing beliefs and customs, saying, "No one sews a piece of unshrunk cloth on an old cloak, for the patch pulls away from the cloak, and a worse tear is made. Neither is new wine put into old wineskins; otherwise, the skins burst, and the wine is spilled, and the skins are ruined, but new wine is put into fresh wineskins, and so both are preserved" (Matt 9:16–17).

This passage describes two common occurrences. Pious people who are steeped in tradition tend to condemn those who differ. Sincere moralists try to make other individuals and groups believe and act just like they do. The ancient Hebrews did this to the prophets. The Pharisees did this to Jesus and his disciples. The Judaizers did this to Paul and his converts, and it's still a real problem for Christians today.

In this case Jesus flatly refused to comply. He didn't yield to their demands or even try to justify his behavior. He realized that acquiescence was impossible. Conformity would have caused him to violate his own conscience. He knew that you can't follow artificial rituals out of duty. You can't obey mindless rules and regulations out of fear. You can't put new cloth on old garments. You can't put new wine in old bottles.

He was emphasizing a crucial insight. Although clean breaks are upsetting and frightening, sometimes they're required. Democracy couldn't be an updated and improved monarchy. It had to be completely different. Sometimes to continue repairing and remodeling an old building is an exercise in futility. If the foundation is rotten and the framework has termite damage, it must be torn down. Jesus knew that sometimes radical change may be necessary and desirable. He foresaw that even his own ministry would bring not peace but division (see Matt 10:34).

Conflict and upheavals are inevitable. The old must go out before the new can come in. Life is a tradeoff. We must give up some things to make room for other things. Christianity is based on these challenging choices. Even the word *repent* means to rethink! As Christians we must commit ourselves to new lives, new priorities, and new directions.

At Vicksburg an engineer showed visitors an almost dry channel. He explained that, once, the great Mississippi River had flowed there, but then workers had dug conduits and diverted it. The flow of the river could not be stopped, but it could be channeled in a new direction. The thrust of our strength, our energy, and our ambition can't be stopped. God doesn't want them stopped, but he does want them channeled in new, positive directions.

What did Jesus mean by the old system, the old cloth, and the old bottles? Well, the old system that he opposed and replaced consisted of rules and regulations. It was motivated by guilt and fear. It was based on retribution and restitution. John the Baptist, who epitomized this system, commanded prospective converts to prove the genuineness of their repentance by their actions, saying, "Bear fruit worthy of repentance" (Matt 3:8). In other words, "Reform, and then God might accept you."

Jesus, on the contrary, who represented the new system, said, "Anyone who comes to me I will never drive away" (John 6:37). In other words, "Come as you are! You'll be accepted even before you reform." This system is based on forgiveness and grace.

The old system said, "The scales must balance. Put in a sin—get out a punishment. Put in a good deed—get out a reward." The rules of justice were absolute and relentless. That's why guilt and fear prevailed. Since you were always making mistakes, you were always coming up short. You were always waiting for the other shoe to drop. You were always expecting the retaliatory evil that was sure to come.

The social consequences were even worse. Since we tend to treat others as we are treated, if God demands retribution and restitution, then so must we. What a terrible life! An eye for an eye, a tooth for a tooth. No hope for mercy, no chance for compassion.

The old bottles are law. The new wine is grace! Grace doesn't require payment. Grace doesn't insist upon a fifty-fifty arrangement. Grace isn't predicated upon a balanced scale.

Jesus told many parables to illustrate this astonishing doctrine, which so contradicted traditional Jewish thought. One of his best stories is that of the debtor: He said the kingdom of heaven may be compared to a king who wished to settle accounts with his slaves. When he had begun to deal with them, there was brought to him one who owed him a large debt. But since he did not have the means to repay, his lord commanded him to be sold. The slave fell down before him and begged for leniency. The lord felt compassion and forgave the debt.

But then that slave went out and found a fellow slave who owed him a small debt. He began to choke him, saying, "Pay back what you owe."

That slave pleaded, "Have patience with me, and I will repay you." He didn't have patience, however. Instead, he threw him in prison until he could pay back what was owed.

When the other slaves saw this, they reported to their lord all that had happened. His lord chastised him and turned him over to be tortured. Jesus concluded with this warning: "So my heavenly Father will also do to every one of you, if you do not forgive your brother or sister from your heart" (Matt 18:35).

In this dramatic story Jesus was suggesting that accounts don't have to balance! Since God doesn't require retribution from us, we must not require it from others. Since God doesn't deal with us on a strict merit basis, we must not deal with others on a strict merit basis. Since God extends limitless grace and forgiveness, so must we.

Paul also advocated free grace. He had persecuted the church and aided those who stoned Stephen, but he said, "Forgetting what lies behind and straining forward to what lies ahead, I press on toward the goal, toward the prize of the heavenly call of God in Christ Jesus" (Phil 3:13–14).

If we keep looking back on our failures, we'll be paralyzed. You can't unsay every deceitful word you've ever spoken. You can't undo every bad deed you've ever done. You can't restore every good thing you've ever spoiled. You can't repay all your moral debts. The old "balanced scale" system is hopeless and demoralizing. All of us come up short when we are weighed against perfection.

There's an anecdote about a man who reluctantly had his picture taken by a local photographer. Upon viewing the print he expressed displeasure. "Oh," said the concerned photographer, "don't you think it does you justice?"

"Justice!" snapped the man. "I didn't want justice. I wanted mercy!"

That's us! We don't want God to respond with absolute justice to all our weaknesses. We want understanding and mercy. Even so, we must not respond with a self-righteous insistence upon justice in every unfortunate encounter we have with our fellow human beings. We must extend mercy and give others the benefit of the doubt.

Love doesn't store up slights. Love doesn't keep track of wrongs received. Love doesn't hold on to resentments! One man, hurrying through a revolving door, bumped into another. He immediately said, "If this is my fault, I'm sorry. If it's yours, it's okay. I don't have time to find out!" What a wonderful, pragmatic way to handle most of life's bumps. We waste valuable time and expend valuable energy making emotional mountains out of insignificant mole hills. We must learn to disregard small slights and overlook minor offenses!

Too many of us carry around a supply of repressed resentments. These seething explosive devices are just waiting for a tiny spark to ignite them. We're disasters waiting to happen. One little imaginary rebuff can set us off! Most of these are in our own negative minds.

Once, a driver had a flat tire in an isolated area. It was about one o'clock in the morning, and his jack wouldn't work. Looking down the road, he saw a farmhouse. He thought the farmer might have a jack he could borrow, but as he started toward the house, he began to think, "All the lights are out. Everybody there is asleep. I'm probably going to make that man angry by knocking on his door at this time of night. I'll wake him up, and even if he has a jack, he'll probably be so furious that he won't let me use it." The scene he created became vivid in his mind. Finally, he reached the farmhouse and knocked on the door. The farmer came to the door, and before he had a chance to say a word, the overwrought motorist shouted, "Oh, just keep your old jack! I don't need it anyway!"

We, too, build our fantasy worlds and then base our actions on them as if they were real. Christian love overlooks a lot. Remember, people need encouragement and acceptance the most when they seem to deserve it the least. We need a helping hand in our moments of weakness, not in our moments of strength. We need a lift when we're down, not when we're triumphant. That's grace! That's the "new wine."

A young man remembers driving the family car on a gravel road and slipping off into a ditch. He said, "The car and I just sat there. I felt so foolish!"

My father turned to me and asked, "What are you going to do?"

"I'm going to get out and let you drive," I replied.

"No you're not," my wise dad said. "You can drive this car. Sit here until you feel better, and then go on and drive."

The young man recalled, "He never mentioned this incident again. He never threw it up to me in moments of anger."

Believe it or not, that's how God responds. In the scripture God declares, "I will forgive their iniquity and remember their sin no more" (Jer 31:34).

God doesn't kick us when we're down. He doesn't say, "Look at you! You're so dumb, so lazy, so worthless." We already feel that way when we're depressed and miserable. We don't need anyone to tell us that. Instead, we need grace! That's the "new wine"!

Often, we're undependable. We're inconsistent. We act like Simon Peter. On the night before Jesus's crucifixion, Peter followed at a safe distance. Later, a young woman said, "You're one of his disciples, aren't you?" Peter replied, "I don't know what you mean." Someone else said, "You are one of his disciples!" Again, Peter said, "I don't know him!" The third time he was accused of being a disciple, he cursed and lied. Then Jesus turned and looked at his frightened disciple, and Simon Peter went away and wept.

Isn't it wonderful that Peter's story doesn't end here? A few weeks after his awful moment of weakness and denial, this same traitor preached a sermon on the day of Pentecost, and thousands of people responded. He knew someone would remember his earlier failure and say, "Who do you think you are to speak to us? Why, you lied and renounced the Lord. Three times you said you didn't even know him, and now you're preaching!"

Fortunately, this didn't threaten Peter. He didn't deny his sin or try to cover up that failure in his life. He didn't excuse it or claim it never happened. That was impossible. Instead, Peter was strong because of what he had done. He could say, "That's right. I did lie and renounce the Lord. Yet now I'm asking you to follow him, specifically because I've discovered that he can love and forgive even sinners like me!"

In fact, we can't really "start over" by abolishing our background and experiences, because we've been shaped by that background and those experiences to be who we are now. Admitting and using them is a far better approach. It's much more effective to build on who we really are—on the good traits and the bad, on the strengths and the weaknesses. That's Jesus's way!

Three times Peter had lied. Finally, he had actually cursed. How would we like to have such behavior reported about us in the newspaper, much less in the New Testament!

When that happened, Peter did exactly what we would do. He wept bitterly! That's better than just wiping the slate clean and saying it never happened. That's better than getting a chance for a new beginning. God worked with Peter as he was, not as he might have pretended to be. Because of that failure, Peter moved on to greater things. This incident helped Peter realize his limitations. It helped him become real and honest. Until that embarrassing episode occurred, Peter had been bluffing, playing a religious game. He had said, in effect, "Lord, don't tell me I'm going to deny you. Look how good I am!" The scriptures described it this way: "Jesus said to them, 'You will all fall away because of me this night.'... Peter said to him, 'Even though I must die with you, I will not deny you'" (Matt 26:31, 35). But he did!

God comes to us in our weakest moments, not in our strongest moments. That's the "new wine"!

God helps us use our failures. Peter was successful partly because he had sinned and experienced a dark moment of the soul. So don't despair when you fall on your face. Don't passively accept the bad breaks of adversity. Use them! They are the building materials for your future. They can help you avoid self-righteousness. They can help you understand others. They can cause you to be more merciful. They can increase your tolerance for your associates and your commitment to God.

God loves sinners! Failures aren't final! The moral scales don't have to balance! That's grace! That's the "new wine"! Don't spill it!

If the scales of justice don't have to balance, what do we do with the problem of sin? Well, there is no concept quite as vivid or universal as the equation of opposition. Kids learn quickly that if something is not good, it's bad; if it's not big, it's little; if it's not up, it's down! These glib little absolute labels are the easiest answers to give. They are the simplest labels to bestow on people and things. They require no discrimination or evaluation. They are satisfying and definite. Therefore, the first and most ingrained vocabulary concepts include these mutually exclusive terms. Unfortunately, this affects our thinking processes.

Now, such opposites are valid to a limited degree, but they can also be misleading. They can set us up for extremism. They can condition us to give irrational, either/or responses that don't serve us well in the real world. Few things are strictly black or white. Few things are purely right or wrong. This seesaw mentality denotes immaturity. If something isn't on the right, it doesn't necessarily have to be on the left. It can be in the center. If something isn't hot, it doesn't necessarily have to be cold. It can be lukewarm. If something isn't in the front, it doesn't necessarily have to be in the back. It can be in the middle.

On and on we could go. Assuming that if it's not totally true, then it's totally false creates great psychological and social dissonance. Full may indeed be the opposite of empty, but there is an infinite variety of possible stages between these two extremes. Old may indeed be the opposite of young, but again there are many years in between.

Saved or lost, heaven or hell, sinner or saint—we're steeped in these thought forms. They fool us. They stymie us. They paralyze us.

Now, the scriptures do mention the narrow road and the wide road (see Matt 7:14), and Jesus did say, "Whoever is not with me is against me" (Matt 12:30). Nevertheless, Jesus recognized exceptions. He had followers, and he had enemies, but he also ministered to large groups that occupied other positions. When his disciples reported that there were those who used his authority but did not identify themselves as his followers, he said, "Do not stop [them]" (Luke 9:50).

We love to categorize and neatly dispose of complex issues. We box people and ideologies into "for us" or "against us" modalities, but this habit can backfire. Many things refuse to conform to our set definitions. Is war right or wrong? Is surgery good or bad? Do guns help or hurt? We have to answer, "Sometimes! Maybe! I don't know!" Most of life's questions are like this. They involve tradeoffs and partial solutions. The conditions and situations must be taken into account and then the least painful or most profitable action chosen.

A good computer is brilliant, but it's also stupid! It can do fantastic things as long as the data is perfect, the information is exact, and the choices are absolute. It is logical and precise, but it has no flexibility or creativity. It can't make allowances for specific situations or adapt to changing circumstances

Laws are wonderful. They can achieve order and productivity as long as the issues are clear-cut, the actions are definite, and the decisions are between right and wrong. But they have no flexibility or creativity. They can't make allowances for specific situations or adapt to changing circumstances. That's why we have trials, juries, judges, and updated legislation.

The Pharisees were computers. They had rules for everything. All actions had to be labeled right or wrong, good or bad, legal or illegal. Unfortunately, this didn't work. It hurt people. It created unnecessary suffering, and it increased misery and guilt. This caused Jesus more problems than nearly anything else. He wasn't a computer. He made allowances for Sabbath regulations. He took human circumstances into consideration, and he adapted religious ceremonies to fit a changing world.

Unfortunately, some Christians seem to have learned nothing from his teachings. Today, many groups are still operating in computer mode. Some of us are still getting hung up on the creeds and rules and formulas that Jesus tried to surpass. We forget that he stressed freedom, saying, "If the Son makes you free, you will be free indeed" (John 8:36).

This old "seesaw" mentality affects our faith. One doctrine that is especially affected is that of God and man. Based on the "theory of opposition," we assume that to put God up, you must put man down. Therefore, if a philosophy like humanism elevates man, then it must automatically diminish God.

There are several fallacies in this assumption: In the first place, the two elements are not opposites. God is in man, and man is in God, so they are not antithetical. Also, if we are God's children, then it's obvious that we must be elevated or diminished together. John said, "Those who say, 'I love God,' and hate a brother or sister are liars, for those who do not love a brother or sister, whom they have seen, cannot love God, whom they have not seen" (1 John 4:20). You can't love God and hate men and women or vice versa.

People with close relationships must be treated equally. For example, do you show reverence and respect for a king by demeaning his son, the prince? Of course not! The king isn't honored and flattered by such behavior. He wants his son revered and respected as he is revered and respected. Therefore, doctrines that try to boost God's sovereignty by emphasizing humankind's depravity are dead wrong. If men are worms, then God is the creator and father of lowly creatures. That doesn't honor God.

Likewise, doctrines that magnify men's and women's worth and possibilities are not thereby subtracting from God's eminence. On the contrary, they are complimenting him as the creator and father of the highest and most valuable species known.

The seesaw mentality has undervalued people. It has put rituals and ceremonies over human concerns. Jesus repudiated this stance. How can a child best honor his parents? By being a beggar? By being a failure? By constantly demeaning himself? Of course not! A son honors his father by achieving excellence; by being successful, by exhibiting self-confidence.

You honor God not by groveling in the dirt or wringing your hands in self-pity, but by being the best person you can possibly be! A family is honored as each of its members rises to noble accomplishments. If even one child fails to reach his potential, the family influence and the father's name is diminished. We glorify God by becoming autonomous, productive, and successful.

The theory of opposition also affects the doctrine of good and evil. These two principles are seen as distinguishable entities. Sins are considered to be "what God hates," and good deeds are "what God loves." Sins are black marks! Good deeds are brownie points! Sins are totally destructive! Good deeds are totally constructive!

Unfortunately, few things can be so precisely defined. This view leads us to overemphasize a handful of overt, easily detected transgressions, such as drunkenness and adultery. It leads us to overlook and excuse the more subtle socially acceptable transgressions, such as pride and covetousness.

Breaking a rule is not necessarily committing a sin. Jesus broke many rules. The scriptures include a strict rule about working on the Sabbath. This rule is even one of the Ten Commandments. But Jesus said there are other things that are more important. If a person is hurting, you should break the rule and help them. Even if an animal is in need, you should break the rule to alleviate its distress (see Luke 13:14–16; 14:5).

Jesus supported his disciples when they broke the rule by gathering grain on the Sabbath. He also reminded his critics that there was a rule about not entering a sacred area of the house of God and eating the special bread. Yet David and his men broke that rule when they were hungry (see Matt 12:1–5).

Jesus was constantly being attacked and criticized for breaking rules. He ate with sinners. He touched lepers. He forgave adulterers. He defended prostitutes. He discussed religion with women. He surprised everyone by praising Mary for her intellectual and spiritual interests rather than Martha for her domestic skills (see Luke 10:40–42).

Jesus talked more about the inward sins of the heart—e.g., hate, lust, and greed—than he did about the outward sins that break rules—e.g., murder, adultery, and theft (see Matt 23:23, 27). He said many rules are just "gnats" (see Matt 23:24).

Breaking a rule is not necessarily committing a sin. Sometimes *not* breaking a rule to achieve a higher good is the sin! In fact, sin is not always an obvious act. It is more often attitudes or character flaws, such as deceit, apathy, and unconcern. Sin permeates and taints even good things. Our motives in matters of charity and service are always mixed. We love both others and ourselves. We work and give, both because of feelings of benevolence and in the desire for praise. Even our best relationships have elements of envy and insecurity.

We can't always delineate our sins. We can't always extricate the good from the bad. Once red and yellow pigments combine, orange results. You can no longer point to the red as red and the yellow as yellow. So it is with sin. It combines with the good in our lives. As the old adage says,

> There is so much good in the worst of us
> And so much bad in the best of us
> That it ill behooves a few of us
> To criticize the rest of us!

As Goethe put it, "It's a shame God only made one man of me. There's material aplenty for both a scoundrel and a saint!"

Finally, the theory of opposition affects the concept of forgiveness. We're accused of permissiveness when we preach a God of love rather than a God of wrath. Traditionalists say, "The theology of free grace doesn't deal with the sin question." They assume that if God doesn't wreak vengeance immediately on lawbreakers, then he must wink at evil. He is seen as either a figure of absolute punitive justice or a weak pushover who is soft on sin! Neither is true.

There are other options. God doesn't demand a pound of flesh. He doesn't send an arbitrary punishment to equal every human mistake, but neither does he pat us on the head and say, "It's okay! I'll overlook your ignorance this time."

No! Not one single sin is ever without its penalty. We do inexorably reap what we sow. The scales do balance in a cosmic sense. The physics law says it well: "For every action there is an opposite and equal reaction." This is true in both the spiritual and the physical realms.

Causes do have effects. Deeds do have consequences. But these are an inherent part of life. They are built in. They aren't always personal punishments or blessings meted out on a case-by-case basis. The whole human family shares collectively in these processes. That's why one individual's laziness or ignorance, no matter how personal he may consider it to be, affects the whole of humanity. That's why one person's vice, no matter how secret it may be, pollutes the spiritual atmosphere for everybody.

All of us are passengers on this planet. We breathe the same air, drink the same water, and consume the same food. We may not meet each other personally. We may be of different cultures, races, and nationalities; nevertheless, we are all on the same earth craft, and whatever happens to that craft affects us all. That's why what you do cannot ever be just your own business. There are no private sins.

God does take evil seriously. God does deal with the sin question. But he doesn't do it negatively and destructively. He doesn't retaliate against us as individuals to balance his almighty scales. Neither does he use Jesus's vicarious suffering as a counterweight to balance those scales. Instead, he deals with sin positively. As the ultimate creator, he salvages all things. He doesn't exact retribution for sin or impose a punishment for sin or require a substitutionary atonement for sin! He does something infinitely better. He utilizes sin! Nothing is wasted in the natural realm, and nothing is wasted in the spiritual realm.

Jesus makes this point in the parable of the wheat and tares. He actually advises his followers to ignore much of the evil around them, saying, "Allow both to grow together," but he also promises that evil will be dealt with eventually and good will triumph (see Matt 13:28–30).

The tares weren't going to be carelessly thrown into the trash fire. Instead, they were going to be bound into bundles because they would be used to provide fuel for poor people. The tares would heat their ovens and be used to bake that very wheat into bread.

Likewise, as the ultimate redeemer, God utilizes all our experiences. He doesn't wantonly destroy the sin in our lives. As the parable says, "This would destroy the good along with the bad."

The fact that sin is used doesn't mean any one of these misfortunes is good in and of itself, but as Paul said, "We know that all things work together for good for those who love God" (Rom 8:28). In other words, the whole can be turned into something positive even though the individual elements are negative.

For instance, it's the purpose of a ship to sail across the seas, but not every part of that ship will even float. The engine, for example, if put on the water by itself, would immediately sink. So would many other parts of the ship. Yet when all the parts are securely fitted together, it does sail. The whole ship can do something positive even though any one individual part might be negative.

A tourist watched a group of students weaving beautiful blankets and rugs. The patterns were colorful and interesting. Each was varied and original. After a while he asked, "When you make a mistake, do you have to cut it out and start over? Does the wrong thread ruin the whole piece?"

"Oh, no!" the students replied. "Our teacher is such a great artist that when we make a mistake, he helps us use it to improve the beauty of the pattern! We work it in as an integral part of the design. That's why every piece is different! We all have our individual eccentricities and weaknesses. These make the products unique and special."

We, too, have our individual eccentricities and weaknesses! We, too, have our own individual strengths and talents. All these woven together makes each of us unique and special.

Furthermore, the scales don't have to balance. Grace has replaced vengeance, and the theory of opposition is not valid. God loves and accepts us as we are. Jesus said, "God did not send the Son into the world to condemn the world but in order that the world might be saved through him" (John 3:17).

He also said, "I came not to judge the world but to save the world" (John 12:47).

This word *saved* means "to be salvaged" as well as "to be rescued and redeemed," so the theology of the church must emphasize that the God we worship epitomizes love, acceptance, and forgiveness. It must avoid vindictive threats of punishment. Its theme must include both doctrines and actions that offer second chances. Rules and regulations must be subordinated to attitudes of understanding and compassion. Its theology must be positive rather than negative. We must follow Paul's advice when he said, "Do not be overcome by evil, but overcome evil with good" (Rom 12:21).

III

The Practices of the Church

For centuries the ever-present human question has been, "How can I get right, stay right, and know I'm right with the fearful unknown?" For many people this means, "How can I hide my blunders, justify my errors, and escape the penalty of my numerous sins?"

This preoccupation with our flaws, failures, and mistakes produces guilt. To alleviate this guilt we try to pass the buck, blame others, and rationalize our negative behavior. All these reactions cause psychological and social conflicts. People are perverse. They need absolution, yet they seek punishment. People say, "Don't blame me," yet they often seem bent upon self-destruction. They boast and brag and bully, yet they really feel unworthy, inadequate, and ashamed.

Most of us have an innate sense of the rightness of the universe. We seem to feel that if we upset the moral balance of life, then bad things are sure to happen. Now, this view is partially correct. Attitudes do have effects. Actions do make a difference. Deeds do have consequences. But hiding or justifying them doesn't help.

This has been a hard lesson for human beings to learn. Our own ignorance, guilt, and inertia make us resentful and critical of others. Primitive people as a whole didn't think or act for themselves. The same universal experiences happened to all of them, yet only a few searched for answers. Only a few refused to accept the illogical and immoral assumptions. Yes, earthquakes and storms and accidents and disease happened, but shrugging them off as the whims of a supernatural deity didn't help. Yes, disasters strike today, but saying, "Well, I guess it was the will of God!" still doesn't help. Saying, "We're just not meant to know," doesn't help either. Instead, we must believe the message Jesus brought when he said, "I do not call you servants any longer, because the servant does not know what the master is doing, but I have called you friends, because I have made known to you everything that I have heard from my Father" (John 15:15).

Religions that teach extreme submission and absolute reliance on God tend to absolve us of our own responsibilities. That's dangerous! As Christians we are children of God. We must think like it! We must act like it! We must live like it!

The church's teachings and practices must emphasize the fact that we are here now as agents of God. Furthermore, as agents we must show concern and provide service to others. Our mission must include lessons and sermons that answer people's questions about developing character, maintaining good relationships, and being productive citizens. It must include activities and projects that help people solve their everyday problems.

We can't afford the sins of apathy and negligence. We can't afford to let things slide. We can't afford to take the path of least resistance. Examine your life. Are you living as befits a child of God?

As Christian men and women we are more than meat and drink. We are more than clothes and cars. We have a spiritual dimension. Are you nourishing and cultivating that area of your life? Are you as concerned about your spiritual poverty as you are about your material poverty? Are you as concerned about your spiritual food as you are about your physical food? Are you as concerned about being clothed in righteousness as you are about being clothed in current fashions? Most of our concerns are so trivial. Our priorities are so superficial; our focus is so shortsighted. Yet Jesus said, "What will it profit them to gain the whole world and forfeit their life?" (Mark 8:36).

Paul said, "Even though our outer nature is wasting away, our inner nature is being renewed day by day" (2 Cor 4:16).

As Christians we have glimpsed the kingdom that Jesus envisioned. Therefore, we must see broader, think deeper, and aim higher. We must live above our circumstances. Jesus proved it can be done and even showed us our own possibilities.

For years, the four-minute mile stood as an "unbreakable" track record. Finally, a man broke that record. A short time later, several other people broke it. Now, runners didn't suddenly become that much faster. Instead, they simply saw it could be done.

Jesus didn't just talk about love. He lived it! His authenticity broke the sin barrier and overcame the depravity barricade. He showed us what can be done! Now we must do it!

Could we accept Jesus as a twenty-first-century personality? Basic problems never change. There are always human needs, social tensions, and superficial religions, but archaic terms and obsolete conditions tend to dull the impact of the gospel. If our lives are to be affected, we must have the courage to get Jesus out of white robes, take him off the donkey, and let him speak to us.

Indeed, if Jesus came today, he probably wouldn't even be considered religious. He was simply too lax on piety! He socialized with undesirable characters (see Matt 11:18–19). He ignored orthodox rules (see Matt 12:1–2). He alienated influential authority figures.

He elevated children and women above preachers and religious leaders (see Matt 21:31; 23:13; Luke 18:17; 21:1–4). In short, he was a troublemaker and a nonconformist!

If taken seriously, Christianity could revolutionize the world! Millions of people, especially the young who are turned off by our churches and institutions, could become enthusiastically turned on to our Christ. Few individuals have dared to explore Jesus's distinctive lifestyle. Cultural conditioning has blurred the original prototype. The artificial formulas and sanctimonious phrases that so monopolize evangelical attention are a far cry from the life-affirming concepts announced by this revolutionary figure!

Going back to the "old-time religion" means going all the way back—past Victorian prudery, past reformation fanaticism, and even past Paul's systematized attempts at application. If we persist, we'll finally discover a man who superseded rules, despised creeds, and refused to define morality codes. He lived freely, abundantly, and productively. And that's the way he wants us to live!

Jesus spent more time on psychological principles than he did on theological doctrines! If we take an honest look at his ministry, we'll find that he totally ignored almost all those things denominations fight about today. He wasted no energy condemning pornography or outlawing prostitution. He gave no religious tests on correct belief systems. Instead, he talked about attitudes, motives, and practical social relationships.

Examining Jesus's gospel shows that our emphases are often exactly opposite to his! We've majored on minors and minored on majors!

Jesus's parables and teachings all concern things that affect our everyday life!

Too many of us believe fairytales that end with, "And they got married and lived happily ever after." But wise couples know that marriage is not the end. It's really just the beginning. Unfortunately, we often present the gospel in this same superficial way. We say, in effect, "And they got saved and lived happily ever after!"

That, too, is a fairytale. Those of us with experience know conversion is not the end. It's really just the beginning. We must not insinuate that one brief encounter with Christ is the final word on the subject. The world legitimately asks, "So you got religion? What next?" Is this a permanent renovation or a temporary whitewash?

Conversion must represent a renovation from the inside, not a whitewash on the outside. Indeed, nothing on the outside can affect the soul of a person. Jesus didn't have access to modern psychological research, but he used modern psychological principles when he criticized hypocritical external facades. He called the self-righteous leaders hypocrites and described them as "whitewashed tombs, which on the outside look beautiful but inside are full of the bones of the dead and of all kinds of uncleanness" (see Matt 23:27).

Jesus wasn't interested in pretense and rhetoric. He was interested in authenticity and action. Likewise, a waiting world isn't interested in pretense and rhetoric. It's interested in authenticity and action. Conversion must make a difference!

Salvation in its true sense opens the gate into freedom. It opens the door into life. We are released to reach our potential. All possibilities are before us. To put it theologically, salvation initiates the process of sanctification.

Sanctification is not a mysterious phenomenon. It's not an emotional high. It's not a pious attainment. Sanctification is simply a natural process. When Jesus said, "Be perfect, therefore, as your heavenly Father is perfect" (Matt 5:48), he was not referring to sinless perfection. The term translated *perfect* means "mature, complete, and whole." Growth is our goal. Salvation allows this growth to begin. Jesus uses the model of physical birth in referring to salvation because the experience moves an organism from a state of inert dependence into a state of active independence. Likewise, when the Holy Spirit within us is activated, we can become both autonomous and self-directive. Our spiritual life develops in stages, just as our physical life does.

Salvation allows all these changes to take place. After a baby is born, it grows. That's axiomatic. Parents, family, and friends would be surprised, worried, and indeed frantic if a child retained its newborn status for five years, ten years, or a lifetime! Yet, too often, individuals seem to stay the same or even regress after their spiritual birth. The church has been lax on this point. We've accepted mediocre lives and half-hearted commitments as the norm. This is a fallacy. Conversion that doesn't make a difference isn't a conversion! It's a whitewash!

Paul said, "If anyone is in Christ, there is a new creation: everything old has passed away; look, new things have come into being!" (2 Cor 5:17).

Let's look at renovations as contrasted with whitewashes: First, renovations are authentic. Whitewashes are fake. When we cover up and try to be somebody we're not, it takes its toll on our energy, destroys our potential, and eventually reveals its deceit. Instead, we need to see ourselves as we really are. We need to accept our weaknesses and acknowledge our sins. Honesty helps us quit rationalizing, lying to ourselves, and blaming circumstances for our failures. We'll no longer criticize others and blame luck or fate for our misfortunes. Renovation demands no pretense, no masks, no facades, no armors, no smokescreens, and no hypocrisy. As the soft drink ad says, "It's the real thing!" That's important!

Once, an art dealer in Italy got a shipment of statues. Some were genuine marble, and some were wax copies. In the cold warehouse it was hard to tell the difference. The shop owner wasn't worried. He said, "It will be easy to separate the real from the fake when they are exposed to heat." He was right. When the pieces were placed in the hot sun, the genuine marble objects remained as stately as ever while the wax copies melted down into blobs. We must answer one question about our Christianity: "Is it the real thing?"

Second, renovations affect the whole person. Whitewashes only affect certain areas. We may go to church more, but our benevolence and generosity remain the same. We may read our Bible more, but our concern for our neighbor's well-being remains the same. Our emotions may be stirred, but if our mental outlook and our behavior patterns are not altered, we'll become artificial and warped.

On the other extreme if we determine to achieve a list of moral reforms without the motive of an intense inner desire, we're involved in a hopeless endeavor. An authentic conversion will change our entire life. The mental, emotional, social, and spiritual aspects of our lives must fit together and enhance one another.

Character conflicts must be eliminated. We don't need excesses of emotion, but neither do we need dutiful performances of good deeds. Instead, we need a balanced lifestyle. Our renovations must be complete, not fragmented and compartmentalized. We need consonance, not dissonance.

Once, a clock began to run erratically. It indicated it was twelve o'clock when it was really six and nine o'clock when it was really three. The owner, in ignorance, removed the hands and took them to a repairman. The expert was exasperated. "Mister, the hands aren't the problem," he said. "I must examine and adjust the inner mechanism, not the outer indicators. These hands are just responding to a fouled-up internal situation." It's the same with us. Our words and deeds are symptoms of our inner condition. Jesus said, "Out of the abundance of the heart the mouth speaks" (Matt 12:34).

Finally, renovations are permanent. Whitewashes are temporary. When we paste on a happy face or add a few new religious words to our vocabulary, they are sure to fade. We can't keep playing the role of a disciple or impersonating the character of a saint. We need a conversion that will last. We need a salvation that will continue to expand. We need a regeneration that will grow. A whitewash job has to be redone every few months to perpetuate the illusion. A renovation will endure. It's true that moods shift and depressions occur, but the overall positive thrust will remain.

Renovation lasts because it's living water, not a stagnant cistern. It's a budding vine, not dead wood. Jesus said, "The water that I will give will become in them a spring of water gushing up to eternal life…. I am the vine; you are the branches. Those who abide in me and I in them bear much fruit" (John 4:14; 15:5).

We are grafted onto the vine. This enables us to draw strength and wisdom and comfort constantly as needed. Renovation is permanent! A tourist stood with a local resident and looked out at the desert in the moonlight. Strange shapes and outlines were everywhere. "How can you tell which are the rocks and which are the shadows" the newcomer asked.

"Oh, that's easy," replied the native. "The rocks will still be there in the morning."

Yes, sometimes it's hard to distinguish the real from the fake, but the real will still be there in the morning.

Another question about our Christianity is, "Will it last?" Jesus said, "The one who endures to the end will be saved" (Matt 10:22).

Today, there's one overriding concern each of us must face. Have we had a spiritual renovation or merely a whitewash? Is our salvation experience real? Is it complete? Is it permanent?

These are the evaluative criteria: Am I sensitive to the Spirit? Do I feel concern for others? Do I love my fellow Christians? Am I truly sorry when I sin?

A man whose feet were amputated explained why it was necessary: "I was caught out in the bitter cold of the far north. As long as my feet gave me pain, I knew I was all right. But when they no longer pained me, I knew they were doomed."

So it is with the Christian. If we commit a wrong or omit a right, we should hurt! That's evidence of an authentic relationship with God.

Also, how do we deal with the sin in our lives? How do we respond to our inadequacies and failures? Individuals with mere whitewashes tend to run from God. They find things wrong with the church. They criticize other Christians. They stop praying. Conversely, individuals who have been genuinely renovated run to God. They want their joy and peace to be restored. They want to enjoy a relationship with the Father that only a realization of forgiveness can bring.

Are we using the spiritual resources God has provided for us? Knowledge isn't enough. Belief isn't enough. Proclamation isn't enough. Admiration isn't enough. Use is essential! We must use the resources God has provided.

Salvation is personal. It's our most important choice. Is it real? Is it complete? Is it permanent? It can be!

Karl Marx charged, "Religion is an opiate of the people!" What did he mean? Do people use religion as a crutch? Do they grab it like a baby does a pacifier? Do they participate in rituals to get the pseudo-highs addicts get from placebos or sugar-pills? Was Marx's criticism legitimate?

Unfortunately, yes, to some degree it was! Religion, like any other powerful ideology, can be used for good or evil. It can lift us to new heights of productivity, or it can lull us into a false lethargy!

We repudiate those who take tranquilizers to escape life's problems. Yet religion can be an effective tranquilizer. It can soothe us into a state of apathy. Many Christian doctrines and expressions ensure this attitude. "Giving our troubles to God" can become a lazy way to avoid responsibility. "Depending on the Lord" can become a euphemism for, "Don't blame me. It's all God's fault." Saying, "I'm acting in God's will," can be used to justify selfish or stubborn behavior. The dangers are evident.

Evangelists who sell religious "snake oil" are despicable. Preachers who urge commitment to Christ to gain material success are antibiblical. Spiritual gurus who promise financial gains in exchange for tithes and offerings are reprehensible. Such false prophets are playing with fire.

God cannot be used! God cannot be bribed! The purpose of our religion is not necessarily to make us happy. It's to make us productive. Happiness is the natural byproduct of a productive life.

The purpose of our religion is not necessarily to make us *feel* good. It's to make us *be* good. Good feelings are the natural byproducts of good character.

The purpose of our religion is not necessarily to make us comfortable. In fact, it should make us uncomfortable in the presence of injustice and mediocrity. Being comfortable is the natural byproduct of achievement and progress.

As the old song says, Jesus never promised anybody a rose garden. In fact, he predicted the opposite. He said, "Expect persecution! Expect disillusionment! Expect criticism!" (see Matt 10:22).

Living any life is hard, but living a Christlike life is even harder. Those who try to go against or ahead of the crowd are bound to encounter violent opposition. People are creatures of habit. They are married to the status quo. Any threat of change is stressful, and normal organisms tend to avoid such stress.

Christianity was never intended to be a pacifier or a tranquilizer. Don't cling to superstitious illusions! Don't hide your head in pious sands! Instead, let your religion enable you rather than enervate you! Let your religion strengthen you rather than weaken you! Let your religion stir your heart rather than ease your mind! To paraphrase John F. Kennedy, "Ask not what God can do for you. Ask what you can do for God!"

Jesus said, "The Son of Man came not to be served but to serve" (Matt 20:28).

Paul said, "It is more blessed to give than to receive" (Acts 20:35).

In the long run a contributive life is a satisfying life, but you must make the effort before you can reap the rewards. You must put something in before you can take something out. No sane person bargains with his automobile, saying, "Car, if you'll take me one hundred miles, I'll put some gas in you." That's ridiculous! That's backwards. Most of us know we must put fuel in before we can get mileage out.

Likewise, no sane person bargains with his fireplace, saying, "Fire, if you'll burn for an hour, I'll put some wood on you." That's ridiculous! That's backwards. We know we must put fuel in before we can get heat back!

Life is like that. It doesn't work backwards. It demands an investment before it will pay a dividend.

People often say, "I'm waiting for my ship to come in." Well, wishful daydreamers might as well forget it. You must send a ship out before you can expect to get one back! Expecting something for nothing is an exercise in futility.

Jesus did not present a gospel of pacifiers and placebos. Now, he did make promises, but he also made demands. Choices always result in tradeoffs. There is no cheap sainthood.

Yes, you can have treasures in heaven, but first you must sell what you have on earth! Jesus said, "If you wish to be perfect, go, sell your possessions, and give the money to the poor, and you will have treasure in heaven; then come, follow me" (Matt 19:21).

Yes, you can own the "pearl of great price," but it will cost you everything else! Jesus said, "The kingdom of heaven is like a merchant in search of fine pearls; on finding one pearl of great value, he went and sold all that he had and bought it" (Matt 13:45–46).

Yes, you can have God's forgiveness, but there's a catch! You must forgive others before you can enjoy this grace. Jesus said, "If you do not forgive others, neither will your Father forgive your trespasses" (Matt 6:15).

Yes, you can be reborn, but first you must die! Jesus said, "Those who try to make their life secure will lose it, but those who lose their life will keep it" (Luke 17:33). In the gospel, crucifixions always precede resurrections.

In every case the rewards of a disciple require the commitments of a disciple!

Sometimes in its zealousness to sell salvation, the church has emphasized the advantages and minimized the disadvantages. Jesus didn't do that. He kept warning people to count the cost of discipleship. He used two everyday examples to illustrate this point, saying, "For which of you, intending to build a tower, does not first sit down and estimate the cost, to see whether he has enough to complete it? Otherwise, when he has laid a foundation and is not able to finish, all who see it will begin to ridicule him, saying, 'This fellow began to build and was not able to finish.' Or what king, going out to wage war against another king, will not sit down first and consider whether he is able with ten thousand to oppose the one who comes against him with twenty thousand?" (Luke 14:28–31).

In other words, don't promise to live out Jesus's life here on earth without careful consideration. Don't claim to be a representative of God's kingdom without serious thought.

Salvation isn't a fire insurance policy. It's a service contract! We are called to work. Jesus said, "My Father is still working, and I also am working" (John 5:17).

Now, this doesn't mean we have to earn God's grace. This doesn't mean we have to work for God's love! This doesn't mean we have to measure up to a certain standard to be accepted by God. It does mean, however, that realizing the benefits of Christianity costs something.

Many years ago, a wise old king called his counselors together and gave them a commission: "I want you to compile the wisdom of the ages. Put it in a book form so we might leave it to posterity."

The scholars left their king and worked for a long period of time. They finally returned with twelve volumes and proudly proclaimed that this truly was "the wisdom of the ages." The king looked at the twelve volumes and said, "Gentlemen, I'm certain this is the wisdom of the ages. It probably contains the knowledge we should leave to mankind. However, it is so long! The people won't read all of that. Condense it."

Again, the men worked long and hard before they returned with only one volume. The king realized it was still too long, so he urged them to condense it some more. Little by little, it was reduced to a single chapter, then to a page, then to a paragraph, and finally to one sentence.

The king was pleased. "Gentlemen," he said, "this is truly the wisdom of the ages, and as soon as all men everywhere learn this truth, most of our problems will be solved." The momentous sentence simply said, "There ain't no free lunch!" And there ain't! Anything of value has a cost!

So what can we expect as Christians?

Jesus said, "You will be hated by all because of my name. But the one who endures to the end will be saved" (Matt 10:22). You will be criticized! You will be judged unfairly! You will be subjected to a double standard of morality! You will be placed in no-win situations! Anything you do will be considered wrong by some factions! You must learn to be your own person, answerable only to God. Jesus said, "If the world hates you, be aware that it hated me before it hated you" (John 15:18).

Paul said, "We are afflicted in every way but not crushed, perplexed but not driven to despair, persecuted but not forsaken, struck down but not destroyed" (2 Cor 4:8–9).

Next, Jesus said, "You have heard that it was said, 'You shall love your neighbor and hate your enemy.' But I say to you: Love your enemies and pray for those who persecute you, so that you may be children of your Father in heaven" (Matt 5:43–45). You will have to exhibit unusual patience. Loving ruthless competitors and extending goodwill to harsh critics is not easy. Those who advocate "cheap grace" have never really tried it.

Then, Jesus gave several warnings about relationship conflicts, saying, "If you are angry with a brother or sister, you will be liable to judgment, and if you insult a brother or sister, you will be liable to the council, and if you say, 'You fool,' you will be liable to the hell of fire" (Matt 5:22). An unbridled temper must be harnessed. Righteous anger must be directed against gross social injustice, not used to prop up our own petty egos.

Jesus said, "Whoever wants to be first must be last of all and servant of all" (Mark 9:35). Self-interest cannot be the only criterion in a Christian's life. The welfare of others must be considered. The overall long-term results must affect our decisions. Even good things can be a hindrance. Pushing for the better and best uses of time and money is a Christian's obligation.

Jesus used a tree to teach a lesson about productivity. He said, "Every tree that does not bear good fruit will be cut down and thrown into the fire. Thus you will know them by their fruits. Not everyone who says to me, 'Lord, Lord,' will enter the kingdom of heaven, but only the one who does the will of my Father in heaven" (see Matt 7:19–21). We must be productive. This is an absolute. Barren ground and fruitless trees are condemned. As Christians we're not admonished simply to be good. We're told to be "good for something"!

Perseverance is essential. Jesus says, "No one who puts a hand to the plow and looks back is fit for the kingdom of God" (Luke 9:62). We're called to follow! Period! Not just until the first hint of opposition or criticism! It's a long haul! It's a marathon! We must persevere! Life is a risk. Any civilization or individual that devotes itself to avoiding all danger and unpleasantness will soon die.

Jesus called different men and women to discipleship. Some responded; some didn't. Jesus had a special attraction to one individual and invited him to be a follower:

> As he was setting out on a journey, a man ran up and knelt before him and asked him, "Good Teacher, what must I do to inherit eternal life?" Jesus said to him, "Why do you call me good? No one is good but God alone. You know the commandments: 'You shall not murder. You shall not commit adultery. You shall not steal. You shall not bear false witness. You shall not defraud. Honor your father and mother.'" He said to him, "Teacher, I have kept all these since my youth." Jesus, looking at him, loved him and said, "You lack one thing; go, sell what you own, and give the money to the poor, and you will have treasure in heaven; then come, follow me." When he heard this, he was shocked and went away grieving, for he had many possessions. (Mark 10:17–22)

We don't know what happened to that rich young man. Maybe he was comfortable and safe for the remainder of his life, but maybe he was bored and unproductive. We do know what happened to Simon Peter. He gave up a lot, and he faced hard choices, but he also had some thrilling experiences and successes.

People can go to Las Vegas and never lose a cent or gain a cent. To do so, however, they must refrain from betting. Life gives us no such choice. We can't just sit and watch it go by. Life compels us to wager on something. It's impossible to live without staking your life on some principle or value.

Jesus never talked of the ease and comfort of the Christian life. Instead, he talked of self-denials and sacrifices: "If any wish to come after me, let them deny themselves and take up their cross and follow me. For those who want to save their life will lose it, and those who lose their life for my sake, and for the sake of the gospel, will save it" (Mark 8:34–35).

Christianity is a challenging adventure! As Jesus's disciples we are not submissive slaves. We are God's special agents. A conversion is a real, complete, and permanent change. It requires a commitment to both righteousness and productivity.

The teachings and practices of the church must include the disadvantages and requirements of the gospel as well as the advantages and benefits. Jesus was honest about the possibilities of persecution and the price we must sometimes pay to live out our faith. The church should spend as much time on Christian living as on evangelism. Character and honesty are paramount, and hypocrisy must be avoided. The church should teach that social relationships are more important than ceremonies and rituals. A successful church provides support, comfort, and strength to its members. Jesus's promise was clear when he said, "I have said this to you so that in me you may have peace. In the world you face persecution, but take courage: I have conquered the world!" (John 16:33).

IV

The Role of the Church

Jesus said, "You will be my witnesses in Jerusalem, in all Judea and Samaria, and to the ends of the earth" (Acts 1:8).

In a media-obsessed world of news, TV, internet, twitter, and bestselling books, the church's and indeed Christianity's credibility is on the line. In light of this, "What manner of people ought we to be?" (see 2 Pet 3:11). Should we be majoring on minors, bickering about trivia, and emphasizing discord? Petty squabbles indicate a "letter of the Law" mentality that lacks spiritual insight into the "weightier matters"! Sometimes Christians can't seem to agree on what constitutes a gnat and what constitutes a camel! In these momentous days, surely a consensus on priorities must be reached. Jesus is our example. Only by analyzing his life can we determine what manner of people we ought to be.

First, we ought to be a people of love! Throughout the Gospels we find this is the greatest emphasis. Unfortunately, the word *love* has been overworked and even cheapened, but we've never found an adequate substitute. Jesus himself used it constantly: "Love me" (see John 14:15); "Love…one another" (see John 13:35); and even "Love your enemies" (see Matt 5:44).

Love is sorely needed in this materialistic age. An encyclopedia in 1768 devoted four lines to the word *atom* and five pages to the word *love*. Two hundred years later, that same encyclopedia devoted several pages to the word *atom* and omitted the word *love* altogether.

Christians must be different. We must exhibit a special kind of love that allows for disagreement, accepts dissent, and respects opposition; a love that truly unifies without demanding conformity; a love that elevates the individual, because the worth of each person is infinite!

Christianity is made for human beings, not human beings for Christianity! Guilt-producing creeds that turn people into neurotic hypocrites are immoral. Promotional schemes that use people as statistics to be manipulated are immoral! Men and women are not puppets, robots, or slaves placed here on earth merely to carry out the whims of an ambitious God! Men and women are valuable not for what they do but for who they are!

Jesus said, "Be merciful, just as your Father is merciful" (Luke 6:36). Mercy suggests compassion and forgiveness. Oh, how we need mercy! The prodigal son's father was merciful. The good Samaritan was merciful. The crucified Jesus was merciful. It's better to pardon too much than to condemn too much.

The scriptures specifically compare the church to the family and the newborn soul to the newborn child. If the family slapped a toddler down every time he stumbled, do you think he'd ever learn to walk? On the contrary, the older members in the family tenderly pick him up, comfort him, and encourage him to try again, knowing full well that more falls will occur. They're to be expected. Yet, too often, the church family sits like a vulture, ready to pounce on new converts at the first sign of weakness. The "babe in Christ" is slapped down by our smug expressions, our critical remarks, and our "holier than thou" attitudes.

To err is human, to forgive divine. We ought to be a people of love and mercy.

You can't fill an empty container with ants by picking them up one at a time. It's impossible! They crawl out faster than you can put them in! If you add a sweet sugar cube to that container, however, it's a different story. They'll swarm in all by themselves. The reason is that you now have something they want. You're filling a need!

Does the church try to attract prospects with empty programs instead of the sweet spirit they crave? If so, we strive in vain! Why do "brush salesmen" have to go out and collar customers with a hard sell while grocery clerks don't? It's because salesmen offer gadgets and grocery stores offer bread! They're filling a need!

Are we offering useless gadgets instead of the "bread of life"? Jesus said, "Feed my sheep" (see John 21:17).

The Bible says, "Let us love not in word or speech but in deed and truth" (1 John 3:18).

Jesus always alleviated physical and mental discomforts. He fed the hungry, healed the sick, counseled the disturbed, and even made wine for an embarrassed host! His concern proves that these "worldly" desires are legitimate. The whole person is sacred!

Jesus broke every traditional rule that didn't serve men and women. He made much of curing disease, which eased human pain, and little of keeping Sabbath-day regulations, which only perpetuated an institution. Every precept Jesus emphasized was to help people, to enrich people, and to inform people. Can we do less?

We ought to be a people of love.

Next, we ought to be a people of wisdom. When Jesus sent his chosen ones to carry out the "great commission," he didn't tell them to be naive illiterates. Instead, he warned, "I am sending you out like sheep into the midst of wolves, so be wise as serpents" (Matt 10:16).

To influence the population of the twenty-first century, we must earn their respect. There is absolutely no virtue in ignorance and incompetence. God wants our best physically and mentally as well as spiritually.

We must forget those things that are behind (see Phil 3:13), because, contrary to popular opinion, "we've always done it that way" is not the first commandment! Things will never again be like the good old days! In fact, they probably never were! Our sighs for a return to the moral standards of yesterday are ill-founded. Sin is not a modern invention. Every age feels that the breakdown of traditions is bringing it to the edge of disaster. Fewer divorces one hundred years ago doesn't prove greater fidelity; it simply means there was greater fear of criticism and more difficulties involved in separation. Less premarital sex didn't result from purer virtues, merely worse consequences and less availability of birth control. Pioneers may have walked to church and sat on hard benches, but what alternative did they have? They had to walk everywhere else, and their homes had hard benches too! Revivals had large crowds because they provided entertainment right along with medicine shows. People don't deserve plaudits for following accepted behavior patterns.

Also, some matters are more consequential than others. We should avoid the temptation to attack a few obvious offenses and evade our responsibility on the more complex problems. Many churches have a great record on passing anti-liquor and drug laws but dubious records on preventing racial discrimination and prejudice! Being lured into innumerable digressions over trivial issues dissipates our energies.

Our moral system has often been inconsistent and downright weird. In fact, morality seems to be in the heart of the evaluator. To some, morality is eliminating abortion; to others, it's providing vitamins for pregnant women.

To some, morality is avoiding premarital sex; to others, it's abolishing capital punishment.

To some, morality is closing gambling casinos; to others, it's advocating gun control.

To some, obscenity means topless dancing; to others, it's torture and violence.

To some, the unspeakable sin is to smoke marijuana; to others, it's to develop nuclear bombs.

To some, having prayer in school glorifies God; to others, limiting the export of weapons glorifies God.

Now, none of these groups is deliberately evil. Each sincerely believes its agenda is the right one. Each is dedicated to a better world. They differ so radically in emphasis and interpretation because their backgrounds, teachings, taboos, and experiences have been different.

Sometimes our values are based on mindless conditioning. Sometimes our values are shaped by illogical propaganda. Sometimes our values are determined by charismatic authority figures.

Let's not automatically condemn those who differ from us on moral issues. Instead, let's weigh matters rationally and objectively.

A generation ago, some Christians said it was wrong for couples to dance to music, but it was perfectly all right for couples to skate to music.

They said it was wrong to go to a movie on Sunday, but it was perfectly all right to watch television on Sunday.

Even today, some preachers rant about those who would break the law and risk lives by drinking and driving but then brag about breaking the law and risking lives by speeding or texting.

Yes, our moral system is confusing at best! Once, a little boy in Sunday school drew a picture of a cowboy entering a saloon. The teacher was horrified until the child quickly explained, "Oh, it's okay ma'am. He's not going in there to drink. He's just going in there to shoot a guy."

Our Lord set a strange precedent in ethical matters. Jerusalem was anything but a holy city in AD 30. Wickedness abounded. Most modern preachers, if put in that situation, would have begun fervent crusades against orgies in Roman baths, alcoholism, and corruption in high places, but Jesus didn't! Instead, he denounced law-abiding, church-going, tithing community leaders, calling them whited sepulchers (see Matt 23:27). How utterly astonishing!

The point is, Jesus never wasted time on symptoms. He went after the disease, saying, "It's not things without, but things within that defile" (see Matt 15:16–20). Sometimes it's more important to deal with the cause rather than merely the effects!

Christians have a positive message, but we often project a negative image. We're "those folks who don't"! We don't drink! We don't gamble! We don't cuss! So what? A newsman covering a religious convention approached a participant and said, "Excuse me, but I've been here for three days, and I've heard over and over what you're against. Please tell me, are you people actually for anything?"

Negation is self-defeating. Jesus took the positive approach because he knew that only righteousness can dispel evil.

We ought to be a people of wisdom.

Finally, we ought to be a people of vision.

The scriptures do present the basis of morality, but specific applications have to be adapted as conditions change. Jesus himself explained this, saying, "I still have many things to say to you, but you cannot bear them now. When the Spirit of truth comes, he will guide you into all the truth" (John 16:12–13).

He knew there were deeper understandings his followers would need as time passed, but they weren't ready for them yet. If he had tried to give detailed instructions for dealing with future issues, such as internet use or space travel, they would have been meaningless. Instead, he stressed underlying values and expected growth to continue under the direction of the Holy Spirit. Comprehending this one point would enable Christians to exhibit maturity rather than frantic hysteria when confronted with the inevitable cultural changes of civilization. Why must we keep weakening our credibility by confusing transient mores with absolute principles?

It's true, the ability to differentiate requires rare judgment, but as we move into a technological world, we must try.

God has also made us agents of reconciliation. Jesus said, "Blessed are the peacemakers" (Matt 5:9). Only Christians can perform this vital task, because those individuals who are only concerned with this world have too much turmoil in their own hearts to spread peace.

We need peacemakers in the home as divorce, child abuse, and drug problems increase. We need peacemakers in industry as strikes and picket lines abound. We need peacemakers on the streets as gang violence, drive-by shootings, and vandalism multiply. We also need peacemakers in the government as war and nuclear destruction threaten.

As peacemakers we must broaden our scope to include brothers in Christ who worship differently, who are more liberal or more conservative than we are. Jesus said, "If they operate in my name, forbid them not" (see Mark 9:38–40).

Christian groups who are attacking and trying to destroy each other don't provide a positive witness. The vital issues today compel us to break down artificial barriers, abolish pseudo-tests of fellowship, and avoid divisive code-phrases.

Christians don't have to be identical. In Greek mythology, Procrustes, a grisly bandit, forced each victim to lie on his bed. If the victim was too short, he was stretched on the rack. If he was too long, his legs were lopped off! Some Christians also insist upon fitting everyone to their own "doctrinal beds." Instead, we should encourage various shades of scriptural interpretation and accept different forms of worship.

Some of us quote, "You must be born from above" (see John 3:7). Others quote, "Just as you did it to one of the least of these brothers and sisters of mine, you did it to me" (see Matt 25:40). Now, these statements are both in the Bible.

Some of us emphasize the plan of salvation. Others emphasize social relationships. They are both important parts of the gospel.

Yes, the Bible says, "By grace you have been saved through faith, and this is not your own doing; it is the gift of God—not the result of works, so that no one may boast" (Eph 2:8–9); but it also says, "A person is justified by works and not by faith alone" (Jas 2:24).

You see, there are many facets to Christianity, and all of them need to be explored. Why can't individuals perceive and reflect those spiritual aspects that are most relevant and significant to them and then be willing to let other people do the same? That's what Paul and James did.

Actually, Paul's advice on differences, even differences about important ethical issues, is surprising. He advises us to welcome any brother or sister who wants to join, even though their faith is weak. We should not criticize people for having different ideas about what is right and wrong. He explained that we should not argue with people about whether or not to eat meat. Some people prefer to eat vegetables rather than meat that's been offered to idols. Those who do eat that meat must not look down on those who won't. Likewise, those who won't must not find fault with those who do. He emphasizes that our fellow Christians are not our servants. They are only responsible to God (see Rom 14:1–13).

Everyone knows that variety provides insurance against total defeat, as well as being "the spice of life." Any thinking person knows that in this complex world, full of complex problems, it's preferable to have several methods and processes and opinions available. The only place where being identical seems to be a virtue is among certain dogmatic religious groups. When everyone must think alike, believe alike, interpret alike, and communicate alike, all creativity is lost. Spiritual clones are notoriously nonproductive.

Diversity was evident in the New Testament. John's theology was quite different from Peter's. Barnabas and Paul openly disagreed over whether Mark should accompany them. The scripture says, "Barnabas wanted to take with them John called Mark. But Paul decided not to take with them one who had deserted them.... The disagreement became so sharp that they parted company" (Acts 15:37–39).

Then, in doctrinal matters, the apostles differ in their teachings. Paul emphasized faith, and James emphasized works.

It's ironic to realize that such a degree of diversity would probably not be tolerated today. James would be condemned because he doesn't mention the death, burial, or resurrection of Christ even once! There is no information about a sacrifice on the cross, the blood of the Lamb, or a new birth! Instead, James expressed the gospel as he saw it, to meet the needs as he saw them.

If doctrine is really so cut and dried, the wide range of views and concepts represented in the scriptures would be unnecessary and misleading. An interpretation of Christianity from just one perspective is inadequate. After an accident in space, NASA begged for videos from everyone who had taken pictures of the event, saying, "In order to understand the whole truth about this situation, we need views from as many directions as possible." The same thing is true of religion. Therefore, we must nurture our cutting-edge theologians. We must encourage our slightly offbeat thinkers. We must not only tolerate but cherish those who hear a different drummer and sing a different melody. They may well hold the answers to the future. We need diversity!

Tolerance is not a vice; it's a virtue! We can be a people of vision because success is assured. Paul said, "Thanks be to God, who gives us the victory" (1 Cor 15:57).

God's will for all Christians is for them to have abundant and successful lives. The church must exemplify a God of love, wisdom, and vision as it ministers in the twenty-first century.

Many people insist that our place of worship must be a "New Testament church," but there's no such thing! Trying to do everything just like the apostles did is both impossible and unreasonable. They had no sound systems, no hymnbooks, no pews, no air conditioning, and often no buildings. They certainly didn't have family centers and electronic devices. In fact, they didn't even have the New Testament.

Some say because Paul told women to be silent in one first-century situation, then that commandment is still universally operative today. But another passage tells slaves to obey their masters (see Col 3:22), and they say, "Oh, that's not applicable now." What's the difference?

New Testament church members sold their property and gave the proceeds to the poor (see Acts 4:34–35), but few modern-day legalists do that! In fact, it's biblical to elect deacons by drawing lots (see Acts 1:26), but no church follows that example. Must we turn all our books into scrolls and throw away all our cellphones in order to be a "New Testament church"?

You see, life progresses. Cultural changes are inevitable, and if we make transient customs into absolute laws, then we are doing exactly what the Pharisees did—"quenching the Spirit." Jesus didn't insist on obeying "Mt. Sinai rules" and using "Mt. Sinai methods." Instead, he advocated putting "new wine in new bottles" (see Matt 9:17). He went beyond the past, and so must we! Adapting to modern life is not being sinful! Paul said, "I have become all things to all people, that I might by all means save some" (1 Cor 9:22).

Christianity is not for fanatics. It's for ordinary men and women! The original gospel emphasized developing character, improving social relationships, and managing our resources in this life. Therefore, the artificial gap we've created between the church and the world must be closed.

The word *church* does not mean an institution or an organization. It means a group of people "called out to learn of Christ and exemplify God."

Jesus said, "If salt has lost its taste, how can its saltiness be restored? It is no longer good for anything…. You are the light of the world. A city built on a hill cannot be hid" (see Matt 5:13–14).

Now, if he were speaking today, he'd probably say, "Flashlights with dead batteries are useless." In fact, they are worse than useless. They are deceitful and destructive. They are worse because we expect them to work. We depend on them. We trust them, and then in moments of crisis, when we need them most, they let us down. We need light, yet we're left in darkness.

All of Jesus's analogies of Christianity and the church include the idea of usefulness. Salt improves flavor. Yeast increases quantity. Light provides knowledge.

Is this a picture of the church today? Do we have dead batteries? Have people expected us to speak, to act, to stand for our convictions, and then in the moment of crisis, have we let them down? The world needs light. Have we left it in darkness?

Maybe we've failed because we've tried to base our religion on what we think God wants instead of what we know people need. The Pharisees did this. They thought God wanted the Sabbath kept absolutely and completely. In order to do so, they neglected the sick and the poor. Jesus reversed this situation, saying, "The Sabbath was made for humankind and not humankind for the Sabbath" (Mark 2:27).

Unfortunately, we didn't learn from his examples. We're still hung up on emphasizing the exact doctrines and rituals that we believe were prescribed by God rather than seeking to fill the obvious needs of the people around us.

Jesus said, "The Son of Man came not to be served but to serve" (Matt 20:28). Likewise, the church is here to serve. The church is not a business that measures its success by statistics. It is not a police force that imposes religious precepts on a community. It is not a court of law that judges, condemns, and sentences the guilty.

The church is a hospital for sinners, not a museum for saints. As a hospital, it must welcome the socially crippled, the emotionally lame, and the morally blind. A hospital doesn't close its doors to those with diseases and handicaps. That would be both foolish and wicked. These very people are its reason for existence. The same is true of the church. Jesus said, "Those who are well have no need a physician but those who are sick; I have come to call not the righteous but sinners to repentance" (Luke 5:31–32).

It's significant that Jesus reached out to the last. He said, "People will come from east and west, from north and south, and take their places at the banquet in the kingdom of God. Indeed, some are last who will be first, and some are first who will be last" (Luke 13:29–30).

Jesus reached out to the least. The scriptures say, "Whoever welcomes this child in my name welcomes me, and whoever welcomes me welcomes the one who sent me, for the least among all of you is the greatest'" (Luke 9:48).

Jesus certainly reached out to the lost. The scripture says, "The Son of Man came to seek out and to save the lost" (Luke 19:10).

Likewise, the church should be open and hospitable because it's God's church. If we're not loving and accepting, then we don't have a right to call ourselves a church. Democracy means, "I'm as good as you are!" Christianity means, "You're as good as I am!"

Yes, we have a mission to the last, the least, and the lost. We must not be prejudiced and snobbish.

It's not the purpose of the church to observe and censure the world from the safe position of a heavenly hill. It's the purpose of the church to interact with humanity and, like leaven, to combine with and transform whatever it touches.

Jesus associated with the "undesirables," saying, "I have not come to call the righteous but sinners" (Matt 9:13).

We tend to get our heads up in the "clouds of glory." Like Peter and John, we prefer the transfiguration experiences on the mountain to the unpleasant problems in the valley.

Is going to church a deadly duty? Is the good news of the gospel being announced in such a way as to cause disappointment and disillusionment? The theoretical teachings of the church are often a thousand miles from the everyday concerns of ordinary people.

It's unfortunate that in areas of wholeness, mental competence, emotional maturity, and social adjustment, there is little apparent difference between members and non-members of the church. Christians have an obligation to promote love, peace, and joy.

Division and strife within the church have done more harm to Jesus's gospel than all the atheism and agnosticism that ever existed!

For years, specialists in aerodynamics wondered why Canadian geese fly only in the "V" formation. Two engineers calculated in a wind-tunnel test what happens in such a formation. They discovered that each goose, in flapping its wings, creates an upward lift for the goose that follows. When all the geese do their part, the whole flock has about a seventy percent greater flying range than if each bird flew alone.

That's the purpose of the church: We're to lift each other up, not push each other down!

Our contrived morality standards often become a barrier to outreach. Many people make one of two responses: They say, "I'm too good! I'm better than the hypocrites who belong to that church." Or "I'm too bad! I could never measure up to their requirements." In either case they miss the infinite joy of being part of a community that accepts them as they are!

Institutions often abuse their influence, and the church is not immune to this danger. Burdening people with guilt tears down self-worth. Forcing views on people undermines freedom of conscience.

It's never wrong to question and explore. Even disagreement is legitimate if it avoids vested interests and prejudice. It's not the mission of the church to make stern pronouncements. It's the mission of the church to stimulate thought and point out new ethical directions.

The church cannot depend upon its past popularity. To get respect today, the church must earn it! This generation won't come to church just because it's the "right thing to do." Attendance from habit is disappearing. "You ought" as a persuader has been conditioned away by television commercials. We've become immune to the hard sell. The "little brown church" is gone. The "sawdust trail" is gone! Dangerous cults have made people suspicious of all those who try to present a formal "witness."

Fortunately, none of these are hindrances to the kind of evangelism Jesus envisioned. Reaching out to the world is not something you *do*; it is something you *are*. Witnessing is personal interaction. People see God through interacting with loving Christians, not through doctrines. Our true role as believers lies in embodying such wholeness of character and joy of life that others will ask for our secret.

At a picnic, one single ant appeared on the table and went straight for the sugar bowl. After eating some bits of sugar, it took a small piece and went off the table, down the leg, through the grass, into a hole. Not long afterward, it returned with several of its relatives. They all climbed the legs of the table, marched along the top, and entered the sugar bowl. After they had eaten their fill, they departed, each with a piece of sugar in its mouth. Soon, a swarm of ants arrived to feast on the sweet stuff. That's evangelism! If we have something others want, they'll come and try to find it. It's our responsibility to help them find it.

Evangelism is a natural outgrowth of the grace that's in us, not a super-pious overlay. Terrifying threats take unfair advantage of people's emotions. Rosy promises appeal to the worst human traits rather than the best. It's been said, "Stars don't blow horns; they just shine!" We tend to say, "Here it is! A creed—all prepared! Take it or leave it!" When they leave it, as they usually do, our typical response is to shrug and declare, "We've done our part! Their blood is off our hands." This graphically reveals that we were more interested in alleviating our own guilt than in promoting the other person's spiritual well-being.

We must allow people to meet God at whatever point they feel a need. If the encounter is genuine, their understanding and commitment will grow and deepen.

Jesus said, "Whoever has seen me has seen the Father" (John 14:9). As Christians, we now stand in his place. Do people who see us in everyday life glimpse the nature of God? That's our purpose! Many modern individuals have never heard God's authentic word. They don't hear it in "theological sermons." They don't hear it in formal "plans of salvation." They only hear Jesus as he speaks through us in ordinary conversation.

We're not told to win individuals to a list of facts. We're not told to evoke dramatic emotional experiences. Instead, we're told to make disciples! This command is often forgotten. It really means we should encourage people to become avid students searching for truth and righteousness.

The church also has the privilege of announcing forgiveness. Jesus said, "If you forgive the sins of any, they are forgiven them; if you retain the sins of any, they are retained" (John 20:23). This means that if the church accepts people and views them as forgiven, they will begin to feel and act forgiven. On the other hand, if the church rejects people and insists upon viewing them from an unforgiven position, they will remain so. In short, the way the church views and treats people is how they will become.

There is no hope if the church doesn't offer it. Christianity, like classical music, needs no defense! It only needs rendition. A wrangling controversy in support of doctrine is like a symphony orchestra beating people over the heads with their violins and trumpets to prove that their music is beautiful. If they would just play it, everyone would know!

So what is the church?

Overall, the church is a fellowship that serves as a spiritual haven for those who hurt physically, mentally, and emotionally. The church is a fellowship that evangelizes by reaching out with comfort and encouragement to a needy community and to a needy world. The church is a fellowship that teaches and makes disciples or learners of all members.

Of course, in every church there are those who want to enjoy the privileges of church membership without assuming the responsibilities of Christian discipleship. During the football season we hear many sideline quarterbacks who sit in the bleachers and tell how the game should be played. Likewise, one of the greatest perils that churches face is from members who want to sit on the sidelines and advise or criticize instead of getting involved.

Two women who had traveled in Europe were swapping stories. "Did you see the church of St. Chapelle?" asked one.

"Yes," answered the other.

"Didn't you think it the most beautiful thing you had ever seen?" asked the first.

The other replied, "Well, I just saw it from the sightseeing bus."

With indignation, the first woman said, "Oh! You can't see it from the outside looking in. You have to see it from the inside looking out."

That's true of the church. It can only be experienced and appreciated from the inside out. Churches must be devoted to love, wisdom, and vision. They must be tolerant, progressive, and adaptable. Above all, they must seek the last, the least, and the lost.

Has the salt of our integrity lost its savor? Has the yeast of our enthusiasm lost its power? Has the light of our lives lost its ability to illuminate?

We need light! The world needs light! We must not operate with dead batteries!

The role of the church is of crucial importance. In the midst of hype and propaganda, people need information and advice. Truth is important, and the church can provide it. In an age of complicated technology and impersonal electronic gadgets, people yearn for intimacy and friendship. Again, the church can provide it. Fellowship is a significant word throughout the scriptures. It includes compassion and social interaction. The early church was described this way: "They devoted themselves to the apostles' teaching and fellowship, to the breaking of bread and the prayers" (Acts 2:42).

V

The Leadership of the Church

The original church was basically a lay fellowship, but most churches today have leaders—ministers, pastors, bishops, elders, priests and preachers. The leader sets the tone and delineates the scope of the church. In most small churches he fills the role of an orator, a counselor, and an administrator. In larger churches there may be several leaders. Since a church leader is looked upon as an example and model of Jesus, he must exemplify certain moral and spiritual characteristics. Above all, pastors must have integrity. It's unfortunate that their sins are often hidden because they are of the spirit rather than of the flesh. Respectable and yet insidious flaws like pride, greed, covetousness, and intolerance are common weaknesses of religious leaders.

Unethical preachers may misquote, slant, and manipulate facts. If they don't agree with an idea or doctrine, they may ridicule it. Some may attack certain controversial theological, philosophical, or scientific concepts when there is no one present to defend them. This is unfair and cowardly behavior.

Instead, truly caring pastors promote harmony and peace. They never take stands or make statements that will polarize their congregations or set one group against another. They never hurl condemnation at rival groups or denominations. They know that denouncing opponents is futile and persuading people who differ doctrinally to love one another is difficult. Even Jesus couldn't get twelve men to sit down together during his last week on earth without petty bickering.

Good pastors realize that congregations are composed of individuals at various stages of development. The shepherd must stay ahead of his sheep but not out of sight! A wise leader doesn't try to standardize his members; instead, he prizes those who have various viewpoints and encourages them to use their unique gifts. The inclusion of different dispositions, opinions, cultures, and theologies helps us avoid deadening uniformity. Rejecting those who don't agree destroys fellowship and robs the church of its vitality.

The temptation to take cheap shortcuts and use easy, expedient methods is great. Also, some leaders seem to feel that the grass is always greener elsewhere. But honorable men are not fickle. They don't toy with churches by using them as steppingstones to bigger and better positions. They don't take credit for their successes and then abandon them when the going gets rough. Such brief, unproductive pastorates hurt both churches and leaders.

Then, the preacher must have competence. The first priority of a preacher is to be a truth-seeker and a truth-teller. He must constantly dig for hidden insights and then translate them into practical, understandable principles.

Some preachers engage in irrelevant and useless arguments over specific scriptures and complex theological questions. Those reformers who spend their time attacking symptoms, like worldly pleasures or heresy, get sidetracked and waste energy. Those who chip off a little fragment of doctrine and use it to form the core of their mission get off balance.

Extreme literalism is another dangerous practice. It has even led to tragedies such as burning witches (see Exod 22:18) and senseless slaughter (see 1 Kgs 18:40). Literalism has been used to justify slavery and to set dates for the "second coming." It pits religion against science. Then, when religion inevitably loses in those confrontations, it thereby loses credibility in all areas. Taking words and sentences out of context also nullifies validity. Every word in the Bible can't be equally authoritative. Jesus updated many passages, such as "an eye for an eye" and "love your friends and hate your enemies."

Furthermore, the scriptures are progressive in knowledge and insight. The earliest writers are not as complete and mature as the later writers. Each writer expressed what he thought was the best advice in his era and culture, but it is not necessarily best for us with our further illumination. Just because something is right at one time doesn't mean it will be right for a later time. We don't make a thirty-year-old man keep wearing the same shoes that fit him perfectly at age three. It's also obvious that some scriptures should be accepted as allegory. Jesus's parables certainly demonstrate that stories can be legitimate analogies for conveying deep truth.

Above all, our theology must elevate people. Jesus's supreme command is to "love your neighbor as yourself." When God said, "I desire mercy and not sacrifice," he meant social relationships must take precedence over creeds and ceremonies. Preachers should present relevant information that will increase freedom, peace, and joy.

Churches must not waste people's time and money. Instead, they should have a well-defined focus and purpose. A good leader assesses needs, plans strategies, and prepares sequences of teaching material. He doesn't organize empty programs or confuse activity with accomplishment. Ministry is usually effective in exact proportion to the quality of its goal.

A minister's job description sometimes encourages him to be vague. Demands are constant, and details are innumerable, but there is no definite supervisor. This makes effective administration and organization even more important.

Sermons should follow a systematic plan for the year, covering all the basic human needs and problems. Choosing random topics on a week-to-week basis will soon degenerate into a narrow list of the pastor's pet peeves.

A preacher must do more than just impart information. Dictionaries, libraries, and the internet can do that! He must open eyes, stretch minds, and inspire people not only to feel but also to think and reason and grow.

Preachers have no right to be mediocre! Irrelevant sermons are much worse than useless! They are irreparably damaging. They alienate and estrange seekers. Good speakers must have a point and present it concisely and clearly in conversational style. Their delivery should be simple and natural. It's obvious that if a preacher can't say it, he doesn't know it! Speaking for God is not the same as performing routines for God!

Finally, the preacher must have humility and tolerance. Arrogant preachers are insufferable. Such leaders set themselves up as ordained authority figures. They don't merely feel called to share their beliefs. Instead, they feel compelled to impose their beliefs on their congregation. Such egotists often act as if anyone who contradicts or disagrees with them is committing spiritual treason. Assuming that people are rebellious and antagonistic is a symptom of such paranoid leaders. Truth can only be proclaimed in love. Mature individuals don't pose as "defenders of the faith"! They know that true faith doesn't have to be defended by self-appointed tyrants. Besides, bitter attacks never work. A shepherd doesn't fight his sheep; he feeds them. The leader's function is to enhance life, not dictate faith.

The smug overlord in the church is more destructive than the heretic. An "orthodox brother" who feels his "orthodoxy" gives him the right to condemn those who differ tramples the greatest commandment under his feet. A pastor can't glorify God and scorn his congregation. A pastor can't serve God and hurt people.

Impatience also wrecks churches. Just because some project is productive doesn't mean it must be instituted before sundown! Even an excellent idea that's forced on people causes so many injuries that its benefits are nullified. Jesus said, "I still have many things to say to you, but you cannot bear them now" (John 16:12).

In doctrine, as in other areas, the temptation to "nail it down and wrap it up" is great. Absolutism brings comfort. It resolves conflicts and allows our minds to shift into neutral. Nevertheless, jumping to premature conclusions and locking yourself into inflexible positions is dangerous. For instance, the early apostles expected the imminent bodily return of Christ. This mistake affected the motivation and methods of the first century. Circumstances change, and religious leaders don't know everything. Paul said, "We know only in part" (see 1 Cor 13:9). Therefore, belief systems should be broad enough to allow for flexibility.

Questioning is not sinful. Jesus stressed reason and rewarded honest doubt. After all, Thomas was not excommunicated for denying the resurrection, and Paul never even mentioned the virgin birth.

Furthermore, since all truth is of God, much valid information inevitably finds its way into other cultures and religions. The principles of Christianity can be found in unlikely places. The scripture says, "All things came into being through him, and without him not one thing came into being" (John 1:3). If God is everywhere and Jesus is "the true light, which enlightens everyone" (John 1:9), then no true insight or moral achievement from any source should be held in contempt.

Since God's grace can appear outside orthodox Christianity, no person should be ridiculed or persecuted as an unbeliever. Remember, God cares about all people and actually supports and strengthens some who don't even know him, He said, "I arm [support and strengthen] you, though you do not know me" (Isa 45:5). Jesus stated the same idea, saying, "I have other sheep that do not belong to this fold. I must bring them also" (John 10:16).

Launching new crusades and denouncing sin can easily be overdone. People can't live on condemnation alone. Even a virtue becomes a vice if it's carried too far!

A church is an organism to be nourished. Hungry sheep must be fed. Success is to be measured by the development of Christlike character and compassionate service, not by the size of buildings, attendance, or offerings. Churches can be rich in money and programs but poor in love and wisdom.

Preachers are shepherds, leaders, and examples. They must exemplify integrity, competence, and tolerance.

Language is also important. "Hearing the gospel" requires more than simply listening to a few proper religious phrases. For communication to take place, verbal statements must connect with reality. We must realize that it takes two to speak truth: a speaker and a listener. If words aren't meaningful to the one who hears them, they're worthless.

For example, a missionary to a southern island said, "Our climate is steamy. We have no wintertime here. The scripture that says, 'Though your sins are like scarlet, they shall be as white as snow' (see Isa 1:18), makes no sense to our people. Instead, we have to say, 'Your sins shall be as white as the inside of a coconut.'" Now, in that particular location, which of these two statements would be truly "inspired"?

Many people today have never heard the gospel because it is spoken in a foreign tongue, namely the "language of Zion." This situation grows steadily worse as each generation moves further and further away from the traditional expressions. We continue to mouth phrases that mean nothing simply because they sound religious. We're afraid to say what we mean in ordinary terms because it might not sound religious.

Remember, Jesus didn't sound religious either. Instead, he found new ways of explaining old truths. His verbal models were fresh and real. They were out of the marketplace and included the vocabulary of the secular world. It's strange that we have now turned these same vivid, concrete illustrations into pious platitudes. In order to speak to this generation, we must simplify. We must tell it like it is. We must avoid sanctified jargon.

Misunderstanding is rampant! Propaganda is rampant! Superstition is rampant! Emotional hype is rampant! People deserve better than this.

Jesus was a pioneer in plain talk. It was said of him, "He taught them as one having authority and not as their scribes" (Matt 7:29). In other words, he made sense. He dealt with practical issues. He affected lives.

Words can be misleading. As the queen in Alice in Wonderland said, "Words can mean whatever you make them mean." The interpretation is up to us since we as human beings assigned those meanings in the first place! It's strange that we coin words, define words, arrange words, and invent a language, then forget that the terms in this "communication device" are our own creations and begin to worship them.

Even the word *word* is an enigma. For most people "God's Word" means the Bible. Yet John said Jesus became the Word: "In the beginning was the Word, and the Word was with God, and the Word was God" (John 1:1).

Now, Jesus certainly didn't *become* the Bible. In fact, he didn't personally write a single verse. It's evident, therefore, that we must redefine "God's Word." The phrase really means "God's truth! God's self-disclosure! God's revelation!"

The Bible can be "God's Word" to us if we receive meaning from it. Jesus can be "God's Word" to us if we receive meaning from his incarnation. Likewise, nature can be God's word. Our conscience can be God's word. Events in our lives can be God's word. In short, anything or anybody that helps us understand spiritual principles or reveals divine insights can become "God's word" to us.

The point is that there's no magic involved. Words in the scriptures are no different from words in the dictionary. Just reading them or carrying them or memorizing them doesn't necessarily make you better unless you apply them. The Bible is a tool to help us live and serve, not a paper and ink item to be worshiped.

Other important ideas are also cloaked in religious jargon. We talk glibly about sin and salvation and heaven and hell without realizing that these terms mean entirely different things to different people. In fact, they mean absolutely nothing to some groups and some cultures. Of course, the universal concepts that these terms represent are vital to all people in all cultures, and they can be discussed non-theologically. But these life principles only become relevant if we are able to find a mutually understandable language.

Sin, for instance, is often used by religious professionals to mean some artificial transgression against some divine commandment. In other words, God decided, quite arbitrarily, that he wanted certain rituals to be carried out and certain other activities to be avoided. For example, Old Testament believers thought they must kill a dove and burn a cow. They thought they must not put meat with milk or wool with linen. Those persons who didn't abide by these strange precepts were thought to be sinning.

Other theologians view sin as any non-submissive attitude or behavior. They believe the natural human characteristics of independence and confidence threaten and anger God because he wants to be worshiped as the supreme being.

Then the word *sin* gets mixed up with Satan, the devil, and demons. These names are primitive personifications of an abstract concept. Since we can't see evil, we try to put it into a body. Some people even add horns and a tail. Sin also gets described as some inherited tendency toward "depravity." It becomes even more technical and farfetched when we view it as the "seed of Adam" or the "fall of man." When we say a native of Eden ate some ancient fruit, it's valid for people to ask, "What does that have to do with me?"

By being so doctrinaire, we fail to communicate. On the other hand, "sin," when it's defined non-theologically, is relevant. It means anything that is harmful on a practical basis. In this light all mistakes and misjudgments are sinful. Anything that fails to support truth and further love is sinful. Anything that is negative and nonproductive is sinful. Anything that hurts people or damages God's creation or hinders kingdom progress is sinful!

The antithesis of sin is salvation. This is an even more nebulous term. Every religion has its code words for this event. Some faiths use words like *enlightenment*, *nirvana*, and *reincarnation*. Christianity uses expressions like *accept Christ*, *make a profession of faith*, or *be converted*. Other synonyms include *justification*, *regeneration*, and *atonement*.

Now, how many people really know what they're talking about with this jargon? Even if the speaker does understand his meaning, it's highly unlikely that all his listeners will understand it in the same way, unless they are from identical backgrounds and denominations.

Again, *salvation*, when it's defined non-theologically, is personal and relevant. It means attaining spiritual health and wholeness.

Salvation is not punching the right button to get into heaven. Saying, "I believe," is not a password that's required to unlock the pearly gates. Salvation is for now! It integrates our character and enables us to become independent, creative human beings. It leads us to the kind of existence that's worth being permanent and having an eternal duration.

Salvation is for life, both physical and spiritual, both for now and for eternity. It removes the barriers and constraints that would restrict the soul to a temporary existence. Salvation is the realization of our unique relationship to God. It enables us to discover our potential and live out our possibilities.

Salvation gives our body consonance so that our immune systems are balanced and functional. It gives our personality value and security so that blustery egotism and self-punishment are unnecessary. It increases our ability to associate with others because we are no longer insecure. If "God is for us," then negative responses from associates won't threaten us.

Salvation is a psychological state. God offers grace, forgiveness, and acceptance to every person, but not every person realizes, understands, and benefits from these gifts. Since we're free agents, we must choose to activate and live out the relationship with God that is ours by divine right!

Heaven is another word that's used loosely. In the scriptures it is associated at various times with *the kingdom, Zion,* and *New Jerusalem.* It is sometimes used interchangeably with *paradise, eternity,* and *immortality.* Pearly gates, golden streets, and angels are common characterizations. *Abraham's bosom* is the Jewish expression that describes the epitome of comfort and care.

In a broader sense heaven means the abstract, spiritual realm, as opposed to strictly earthly matters. Transcendent concepts are heavenly concepts. The principles of truth and love are heavenly principles. Instead of spending so much time fantasizing about the wings and clouds and harps and thrones of the future, Christians should begin to develop the kind of interests and concerns that can transfer into a spiritual era. We should be devoting our energy to productive accomplishments that will endure in a heavenly environment.

The antithesis of heaven is hell. This is another emotionally loaded term that is often too narrowly defined. Hell has been identified with the Hebrew word *Sheol,* which means "the realm of the dead." This expression has no connotation of reward or punishment. It simply means the state of death.

Hell has also been referred to as *Gehenna.* This name came from the garbage pit outside the walls of Jerusalem where fires burned continuously to purify decay and disease and obliterate the useless waste products of the city.

Many other models are used, such as *lake of fire* and *outer darkness.* Incidentally, these two, if taken literally, are mutually exclusive since fire gives off light and is incongruous with an absolutely black void. Of course, they were never meant to be taken literally.

We cannot conceive of or describe the spiritual negative that is represented by the word *hell. Death, destruction, loss,* and *perdition* are all theological synonyms. They try to convey the awesome concept of spiritual and moral bankruptcy.

The doctrine rests on the assumption that everything has an equal opposite. If there is goodm then there has to be evil. If there is life, then there has to be death. If there is an ideal state, which preserves that which is valid, then there has to be an opposite state, which obliterates that which is invalid.

Bible scholars must admit that details on these and similar subjects are not clear. Contrary to what some avid traditionalists teach, there is no absolute biblical doctrine of heaven and hell. The scriptural writers struggled, just as we do, with ideas that were beyond their human comprehension. Our knowledge is still fragmented. Our comprehension is still limited. Our vocabulary is still inadequate. Therefore, debates and arguments in these areas are futile.

Western civilization, and America in particular, often seem to idolize words, terms, phrases, and labels. We're prone to defend and worship verbal doctrines about God rather than God himself.

Since language becomes obsolete, it can't be divine. Since language fails to cross ethnic barriers, it can't be divine. Since language lends itself to various individual interpretations, it can't be divine. Language is merely one method that human beings have devised to describe and explain things. Our religious language must be as real and clear and honest as possible; more importantly, our lives must be real and clear and honest.

In a European village several centuries ago, a nobleman wondered what legacy he could leave his townspeople. Finally, he decided to build a church. The plans for the church were kept secret. When it was completed, the people gathered and marveled at its beauty. But one astute observer inquired, "Where are the lamps? How will the church be lighted?"

The nobleman pointed to some wall brackets and then gave each family a lantern. "You'll bring these to worship services," he explained. "Each time you are here, the area where you sit will be lighted, and each time you are not here, that area will be dark."

He was trying to illustrate the fact that people may misunderstand our terminology, but they will not misunderstand the light and love that are in us. Character and words must match. Church leaders must have wisdom to share and truth to impart. They must have their priorities in order. Jesus dismissed trivial matters by calling them "gnats."

Instead of wrangling over details, leaders must feed people by emphasizing basic personal and relationship issues that are useful in daily life.

An old farmer attended a church convention. He chuckled as he read the subjects listed in the bulletin. "Look here, Preacher," he said, pointing to the program. "One thing always amuses me about the way you folks do this 'church business.' You've had sermons and talks all day long on how to get people to attend church. But when I go to a farmers' convention, I've never heard a single speech on how to get those cows or pigs to come up to the trough. Instead, we spend all our time learning what to put in that trough. We try to decide on the best kind of feed! I sorta have a notion that if you put more time on discussing what food to put in the trough, you wouldn't have to spend all that time on how to get folks to come to church!"

Are we really feeding the sheep? Furthermore, what are we feeding them?

Paul says he was often reduced to handing out bottles of milk to spiritual babies. He explained that he couldn't speak to them as adults but instead had to treat them as infants, giving them milk instead of solid food. He said the people showed they were childish and immature by their jealousy and petty quarrels and divisions (see 1 Cor 3:1–3).

The writer of Hebrews also used milk to symbolize the watered-down, non-nourishing religious snacks that some weak Christians insisted upon eating. He said, "Though by this time you ought to be teachers, you need someone to teach you again the basic elements of the oracles of God. You need milk, not solid food, for everyone who lives on milk, being still an infant, is unskilled in the word of righteousness. But solid food is for the mature, for those whose faculties have been trained by practice to distinguish good from evil" (Heb 5:12–14).

Solid food must be nourishing. "Junk food," like candy, not only fails to nourish; it gives a false feeling of satisfaction. Those who eat it are no longer hungry and thus could die of malnutrition!

Jesus wasn't speaking lightly when he told Peter to feed his sheep. He knew good food is necessary for health and growth.

Now, it's significant that Jesus didn't say, "Entertain my sheep!" Hiring dazzling performers, professional musicians, and eloquent orators doesn't edify the members or glorify the Lord. The church is not a religious night club. God won't judge us by our Nielsen ratings!

When Jesus said, "Feed my sheep," he meant meat and potatoes, not cotton candy! We are not told to hype people into an emotional state. We're not told to deal with exciting prophecy fads and sensational occult subjects. It's easy to attract people with the miraculous, the intriguing, and the puzzling. If it's weird or different, it has appeal; unfortunately, these are not life-sustaining themes.

Both Jesus and Paul avoided "offbeat," exotic subjects. Jesus criticized those who followed in hope of seeing signs! When the Pharisees and Sadducees dared him to show them a sign from heaven, he answered and said, "When it is evening, you say, 'It will be fair weather, for the sky is red.' And in the morning, 'It will be stormy today, for the sky is red and threatening.' You know how to interpret the appearance of the sky, but you cannot interpret the signs of the times. An evil and adulterous generation asks for a sign, but no sign will be given to it" (Matt 16:2–4).

Paul said tongues and eloquent oratory are much less important than simple kindness and concern: "If I speak in the tongues of mortals and of angels but do not have love, I am a noisy gong or a clanging cymbal" (1 Cor 13:1).

When a baby is hungry, you can distract him momentarily with a noisy rattle or a colorful puppet, but such baubles won't nourish him or satisfy him permanently. The baby needs a balanced diet of good food, and so does the Christian. We're to feed the sheep—not entertain them!

It's also significant that Jesus didn't say, "Pacify my sheep!" Unctuous tones, trite statements, and mindless rituals don't edify the members or glorify the Lord. The church is not a spa or a massage parlor. We're not told to induce hypnotic trances. When Jesus said, "Feed my sheep," he meant meat and potatoes, not cough drops and tranquilizers.

We're not told to lull the people into a complacent state! We're not told to repeat soothing ceremonies or intone traditional platitudes. It's easy to fool people with pleasant, shallow, superficial reassurances. If it's familiar and comforting, it has appeal; unfortunately, these are not life-sustaining principles.

"Everybody loves everybody!" "This is the best of all possible worlds!" or "Just do the best you can!" are not helpful expressions. Sometimes in an understandable reaction against those who give angry, fanatical tirades, certain "happy-talk" groups tend to voice syrupy "positive outlooks." They have an "everything will come out all right" philosophy. These are delusive pipedreams!

Again, both Jesus and Paul avoided them. They were realists who told it like it was and often shocked and antagonized people with their nontraditional and disturbing messages.

When a baby is hungry, you can give him a pacifier. When a child has strep throat, you can give him a cough drop. When a person is guilty or anxious, you can give him tranquilizers. But these things won't solve the problems. Pretty soon, the baby will realize his stomach is still empty. The child will realize he still has fever and pain. The person will realize he's still nervous or depressed. The baby needs a balanced diet of good food, and so does the Christian. We're to feed the sheep, not pacify them.

It's also significant that Jesus didn't say, "Punish my sheep." Causing guilt and creating fear don't edify the members or glorify the Lord. The church is not a courtroom or a prison cell.

Some people are so sick psychologically that they think for medicine to do any good, it has to taste bad! They don't feel like they've been to church or had a worship experience unless the preacher "steps on their toes." They confuse guilt and fear with righteousness.

When Jesus said, "Feed my sheep," he meant meat and potatoes, not bitter medicine. We aren't told to criticize or condemn or threaten. This never effects change. Attacks only make people more inflexible. Aggressive behavior only makes people more set in their ways. You can't force people to change.

A savior rescues, salvages, and heals. That's exactly opposite to the roles of policemen, judges, and executioners.

Since punishment must come after the fact, it's useless in redemption. The church deals in prevention rather than revenge. Besides, the inherent consequences of evil deeds provide their own punishment. The church doesn't need to impose additional punishment.

When a baby is hungry, you can yell at him or spank him, and he may quit crying momentarily, but you haven't filled his need. In fact, you've increased his need. He's still hungry, but now he's also frightened and hurt and confused! We're to feed the sheep, not punish them.

Now, if we're not to "entertain people," "pacify people," or "punish people," what are we to do?

The mission of the church is so important that Jesus repeated it three times. He said, "Feed my sheep" (see John 21:15–17).

How, then, do you feed people? What is the "bread of life"?

To really feed someone you must give them what they need, not necessarily what they want! As long as we want entertainment, pacification, or punishment, we're childish and immature, and as long as leaders and institutions cater to such unworthy wants, they are perpetuating immaturity. Too often, the church is guilty of neglecting and starving the sheep. Too often, the church is guilty of spiritual abuse!

A good leader is one who can persuade and develop people to the point that they want what they need! That's maturity!

Mature Christians crave spiritual food. Fortunately, Jesus explained what food was to him. He said, "I have food to eat that you do not know about.... My food is to do the will of him who sent me and to complete his work" (John 4:32, 34).

Our "food" is to learn, to grow, and to achieve. We may want chips and dips, but we need spinach! Malnourishment makes us apathetic, weak, and subject to illnesses. Christians need food that gives energy, strength, and endurance. There is much work to be done.

A forty-year-old man lying in a crib nursing a bottle is a tragedy. A forty-year-old Christian sitting in a church pew demanding traditional platitudes is a worse tragedy!

As Christians we need information. This includes knowledge. Many church members are woefully ignorant. When one man was asked about the Epistles, he answered, "I think they were the wives of the apostles." We need deep, systematic "Bible study." In short, we need spiritual education. We need to develop logic and thinking skills.

Unfortunately, it's always easier to convert "sinners" than it is to make "disciples."

As Christians we also need affirmation. We need assurance, security, and confidence. We can't serve others unless we're at peace with ourselves.

On airplanes we're always instructed to put our own oxygen masks on before we try to help our children or associates. It's the same with sharing the gospel. We can't help anyone else unless our own needs are filled.

As Christians we need motivation. We need practical applications of what to do and how to do it! Our behavior must match our ideals.

These are the foods of the spirit. If the church leader is to accomplish God's purposes, he must help us do these things. Pastors must be authentic, honest, and competent. They must truly care for their congregations and never use or manipulate them. They must be seekers and teachers of truth. It's not their purpose to entertain, pacify, or punish their flock. Jesus said, "Feed them!"

Peter summarized the "job description" of a good minister, saying, "Tend the flock of God that is in your charge…not under compulsion but willingly, as God would have you do it, not for sordid gain but eagerly. Do not lord it over those in your charge, but be examples to the flock" (1 Pet 5:2–3).

The church needs leaders with integrity and wisdom. These leaders need to use a simple yet wise language style that deals with personal development, social relationships, and spiritual commitment. They need to teach, comfort, and challenge their congregations.

It's significant that one of Jesus's final commands was to Peter, and it was repeated three times. These vital words were, "Feed my sheep" (see John 21:16–17).

VI

The Challenge of the Church

Today, we are being overwhelmed by ideas, opinions, beliefs, and propaganda. An endless number of religions, churches, cults, and other groups seek our support. We live in a world of innumerable worship options, ethical choices, and moral dilemmas.

Which are "right," and which are "wrong"? That's the ever-present question. Unfortunately, this question often has no obvious answer. Not all villains wear black hats! Not all good guys wear white hats! The old Western movies made it too easy. Jesus told the parable of the "wheat and tares" because he knew that at certain stages of development and under certain circumstances, good and evil can look almost exactly alike. Furthermore, trying to separate them prematurely could easily destroy the good along with the evil.

Life is complicated, and moral lines can be blurred, so if we can't pick out the undesirable elements without uprooting the desirable ones, what can we do? How can we distinguish the good from the evil? How can we make the right decisions? How can we make the best choices? Throughout his ministry and again at the very end of his life, Jesus faced the question of moral priorities. He based his life principles on eternal truth, universal justice, and unconditional love. By evaluating his actions the church can increase its own ability to exercise discretion.

Even so, one principle is evident: Few decisions will be between clear-cut alternatives. Instead, Christians usually face the much more difficult task of choosing between good and better. For instance, should members of certain sects be forced to seek medical attention for their children against their beliefs? This involves the question of which is more important—a specific child's life or the overall principle of religious freedom? There is no one correct response.

Christians can even be forced into the absolutely no-win situation of having to select the lesser of two evils. For instance, when terrorists hold hostages for ransom, should we pay and secure their release or refuse to pay and let them kill the innocent victims? This pits an immediate evil result—death for a limited number of persons—against a long-term evil result—the encouragement of repeated violence against untold numbers of victims. Again, there is no ideal solution—only bad or worse.

Furthermore, even the most appropriate choices made under the best of conditions may not be perfect! We simply can't know everything; that entails Godlike omniscience. We can't do everything; that requires Godlike omnipotence. We can't be everywhere at once; that demands Godlike omnipresence. The fact that we aren't omniscient, omnipotent, or omnipresent makes errors in judgment and undesirable tradeoffs inevitable. However, the realization that results are usually mixed must not keep us from trying.

Things are changing faster and faster each day. The multiplying effect is one of the most stupendous processes in the world. They say that a penny doubled each day would become a billion dollars in a few weeks. The same principle is illustrated in the fairytale about the frustrating tree that grew two limbs to replace every one that was cut off. There is also a frightening fantasy of being in a maze of tunnels that reveals two closed doors every time one is opened.

These analogies represent a picture of life in our times. Options are proliferating at a dizzying rate. Every time one decision is made, the information gained creates a dozen new quandaries to take its place. Every time one problem is solved, the very procedure of solution throws light on a hundred more questions to be answered.

We're in the midst of a mind-boggling knowledge explosion. Every fact releases a torrent of material. Furthermore, things won't get easier or simpler. They will inevitably become more difficult and more complex. Once, there was bread. Now we have whole wheat, rye, white, sourdough, and dozens more. All of these are available in loaves, buns, sliced, unsliced, and so on. Two or three TV channels became twenty or thirty, and then cable and satellites added hundreds.

Besides this, the results of our decisions have become more consequential, and the effects of our decisions have become more dangerous. As greater amounts of knowledge and power are transferred to humankind, the possibilities for both good and evil are staggering.

We are free to choose, and we can't evade our responsibilities. We have our five senses with which to test reality, and we have a brain with which to reason and analyze. Paul said, "Test everything; hold fast to what is good" (1 Thess 5:21).

We must realize that the same evil occurs, whether our poor decisions arise from ignorance, weakness, or deliberate rebellion. Nature doesn't play favorites and give exceptions for sincerity. What a person sows, he reaps! The consequences are built in and irreversible. A child dies from poison that is given accidentally just as quickly as from poison that is given intentionally.

Even so, it's obvious that blatant, vicious sin is not an inherent trait of the human family. Most of us don't feel a constant urge to commit horrendous crimes. Most of us don't desire to kill our associates or even our enemies. Most of us don't really want to lie and steal and be unfaithful to our loved ones.

The doctrine of man's depravity has been misinterpreted. We know we're not like that, and we know our neighbors aren't like that. Human beings, in the main, aren't creatures of violence and deception. If we were, the species would not have survived. Yet we are prone to sin if we define sin more realistically.

Theologians have been trying for centuries to find the root sin. Some have said, "The cardinal sin is pride." Pride, however, is a strawman. It doesn't actually exist. Self-preservation is the basic instinct that motivates the behavior we call pride. In our vain attempt to cover up insecurities and measure up to standards of perfection, we act out a role of egotism that is labeled pride but is a mask. Most of us don't even feel adequate, much less superior.

Other theologians have said, "The cardinal sin is rebellion against God." Rebellion is another strawman. The drive for personal maturity and control is the basic instinct that motivates the behavior we call rebellion. In our misguided attempts to become autonomous and prove that we can make it on our own, we act out a role of hostility, but it's a farce! We really don't feel competent enough to be independent, much less invincible.

The cardinal sin is something much less dramatic than pride or rebellion. It's much less overt and much less obvious. The besetting sin of the universe encompasses the principle that science commonly expresses as the law of inertia: A moving body will continue to move. A static body will remain static. In other words, organisms tend to follow the path of least resistance. Jesus called it "fruitlessness." Some of his harshest words were to the tree that didn't bear (see Matt 7:19), the seed that didn't sprout, and the man who didn't invest his talent (see Matt 25:28–30). James said, "Anyone, then, who knows the right thing to do and fails to do it commits sin" (Jas 4:17).

Therefore, we are sinners not because we are so bad but rather because we don't live up to our potential for good. We are sinners not because we commit the big crimes but because we neglect the little virtues.

Issue after issue, the majority of people fall back on the old excuse: "Well, I just never thought of that." Why not? It's our job to analyze life and evaluate facts. It's our job to think of incongruities. It's our job to discover invalidities. Paul said, "Do your best to present yourself to God as one approved by him, a worker who has no need to be ashamed" (2 Tim 2:15).

We are also sinners because we blindly follow charismatic leaders. Over and over, we see people parroting some authority figure or accepting some popular assumption. When confronted, they fall back on another old excuse: "Well, everybody else was doing it, and I didn't want to rock the boat." Why not? It's our job to examine situations and make personal commitments. It's our job to transform the world, not to be conformed to it. Paul said, "Do not be conformed to this age, but be transformed by the renewing of your minds, so that you may discern what is the will of God—what is good and acceptable and perfect" (Rom 12:2).

We are sinners because we take the easy road. In one choice after another, we see people exerting the minimum effort and floating with the tide. An old-time traveling salesman was asked how he chose his route each day. He replied, "Well, you see, I just always walked with the wind at my back." In other words, he never bucked the crowd or swam upstream. Why not? It's our job to change, shape, and use circumstances! Paul said, "We must no longer be children, tossed to and fro and blown about by every wind of doctrine by people's trickery, by their craftiness in deceitful scheming; but speaking the truth in love, we must grow up in every way into him who is the head, into Christ" (Eph 4:14–15).

Yes, establishing moral priorities in all areas of life is essential in a complicated and volatile world. As to religion, remember this: All areas of life are sacred. We must overcome ignorance and impotence. Not knowing doesn't exonerate us from our responsibilities. "What you don't know won't hurt you" is a fallacious statement in a world of drugs, explosives, and nuclear weapons. We can no longer cover our eyes and "see no evil." It exists.

Likewise, incompetence and lack of ability are unacceptable as excuses. We must say, "Lord, we are able, or else make us able!" Apathy and inertia are inexcusable. The world has no place for "deadbeats." Jesus said of the barren tree, "Cut it down! Why should it be wasting the soil?" (Luke 13:7). Unfruitful trees or unfaithful individuals must be and will be replaced with energetic and productive ones.

As to evil, if Christians will recognize and cultivate the wheat, the weeds will die out. We are to do God's will, effect his purposes, and influence his world. Our small contributions can make a big difference. The old adage is true: "All it takes for evil to triumph is for good men to do nothing." Furthermore, James said tells us it is a sin to do nothing (see Jas 4:17).

The world won't wait. We must meet the challenge or perish! The Christians of this generation will determine which it will be!

"Painting ourselves into corners" has come to mean setting up no-win situations. In other words, if you've gotten yourself into such a predicament that any decision you make will be less than desirable, then you've "painted yourself into a corner." Remember, there are no right, good, or nondestructive exits from those corners.

Has the church painted itself into a corner? Is Christianity committed to doctrines and practices that won't work? Has religion developed a theology that has inherent incongruities? As traditional Christians are we in a no-win situation?

Unfortunately, in some areas we have done this. The problems and paradoxes of our faith are becoming insurmountable. A TV commentator said, "Bible Belt believers have one slogan: 'We're against sin, science, and liberals.'" This is indefensible! In the twenty-first century the church is challenged to confess its sins, correct its failures, acknowledge its weaknesses, and maximize its strengths.

Let's evaluate ourselves and our beliefs as objectively as we evaluate other religions and their beliefs. Let's be as critical of our own ideologies as we are of other groups' ideologies. Let's be honest, and let's be fair. We've denied our own inconsistencies and glossed over our own imperfections for far too long.

Christianity can paint itself into corners and become destructive in several ways: First, and most obviously, religion can spawn con artists and charlatans. The very nature of religion makes it vulnerable to manipulation. Since it deals with emotions, guilt, and fears, it's especially susceptible to being used by fraudulent politicians and high-pressure salesmen.

To meet this challenge, as Christians we must treat other people with respect. We must be careful to avoid vested interests. We must remember that we are servants, not dictators. Even Jesus came to serve, not to be served. He never used high-pressure tactics. It's unfair to take advantage of people when they are desperate for help.

Religion also tends to get "set." Since it has claimed to be inerrant, it's reluctant to change. Since it's tied to sacred writings, rules, and ceremonies, it often refuses to revise its teachings or adapt its practices.

To meet this challenge we must be both conservative and radical. We must be conservative in keeping what is good and valid, but we must be equally ruthless in abandoning those traditions and attitudes that prove to be useless and destructive. Holding on to something out of habit is nonproductive. Just because a belief or a method of operation served well at one period of time doesn't mean it will continue to serve that purpose indefinitely. Once upon a time, we needed gas lights and horse-drawn buggies. They were wonderful inventions in their day, but now that we're beyond them technologically, it would be senseless to insist upon their continued use.

Jesus sent the disciples out two by two with staffs and sandals and an oral message. That was an effective and practical outreach method then, but it may not be the best method today. Holding the twenty-first-century church to first-century customs is a misguided attempt at orthodoxy.

Then, too often, religion encourages extremism. A conscience without knowledge and common sense tends to be fanatical. As we become more and more devout, our range of concern and understanding may get narrower and narrower. Religious people can become so paranoid and egotistical that they are like the pious man who wrote a book titled *The Three Best Christians in the World and How I Converted the Other Two!* One musical group sang a song in which they admitted, "We're so heavenly minded, we're of no earthly good!"

To meet the challenge of extremism, we must work on broadening our views and widening our horizons. We should never be afraid of new truths and different perspectives. More information can only enhance our faith if that faith is authentic in the first place.

Religion also tends to foster intolerance. We often say, "I'm right, so if you're different, you must be wrong." The more sincere and dedicated I am, the more tempting it becomes for me to persecute those who differ. I may feel that it's my duty to impose my beliefs on others and force them to conform to my standards. In fact, some people love their god so much, they feel obligated to kill anyone who doesn't!

Jesus's indictment is still true: "Woe to you, scribes and Pharisees, hypocrites! For you cross sea and land to make a single convert, and you make the new convert twice as much a child of hell as yourselves" (Matt 23:15).

Groups who think they have all the answers often become overzealous religious theocracies. Even the apostles and biblical writers knew their limitations. Paul admitted his inadequacies, saying, "For now we see only a reflection, as in a mirror, but then we will see face to face. Now I know only in part; then I will know fully, even as I have been fully known" (1 Cor 13:12). It's easy for people who think they have a perfect understanding of the Bible to become insufferable perfectionists!

Hitler envisioned a pure race. This outlook is especially dangerous because the sicker these people become, the more fanatical they become. And the more fanatical they become, the sicker they become.

They are deaf to the truth and unable to recognize their own faults. They have convinced themselves they are God's gift to the universe.

To meet this challenge we must keep open minds. We must realize that there are many ways of seeing things. We must recognize that if something is different, it isn't necessarily wrong. Two plus two is four, but so are three plus one and nine minus five. Furthermore, what's right for me may not be right for you! Truth isn't single-faceted. It's a "many splendored thing"!

God's concern for us is that we become whole, productive people. How we do that is determined by our special needs and dispositions rather than by some predetermined divine decree. That's why there are many diverse salvation experiences. The type of understanding and transformation that's liberating for me may be totally ineffective for you. We're individuals. We must let each person discover and work out his own redemptive process. That's what Paul suggests (see Phil 2:12–13). The method is not wrong if it produces a regenerated and transformed life. Jesus gave each person specific advice and special attention.

Intolerance is unchristian. It's easy to love our family, but someone needs to love the unlovely, homeless derelict. If Christians don't, who will? It's easy to love America, but someone needs to love Iran and North Korea. If Christians don't, who will?

It's unfortunate that religion has often degenerated into superstition. A little piece of truth that becomes twisted is deadly! Too often, we worship beliefs *about* God instead of God! We create idols out of virtues. We let our emotions overrule our reason. Religion taps into the deepest innermost parts of a person. That's why a little theology is a dangerous thing. We can have just enough religion to make us miserable and hostile and not enough to make us happy and helpful.

In these areas, if wisdom and honesty don't prevail, silly tangents and nonessential concepts can become sacred formulas. There's no nonsense so outrageous as religious nonsense. That's why Jesus said, we must be "as wise as serpents." To meet this challenge we must understand that just because something is religious, that doesn't make it true. Lies dressed up in sanctimonious language are still lies. Ignorance masquerading as "blind faith" is still ignorance. Don't be fooled!

Also, just because something is popular doesn't make it valid! What would happen if everyone voted to repeal the law of gravity? Well, nothing would happen! Our action would just expose our ignorance. We do not control truth; truth controls us!

There is even danger today of religion becoming irrelevant. Often, we spend so much time on long-ago events or improbable future scenarios that we neglect the less sensational problems. It's obvious that modern men and women don't rush to church every Sunday with eager anticipation to hear about the ancient Jebusites. Unless a subject affects us, no learning takes place. To meet this challenge we must discover real human needs and fill them. We must be sure our ceremonies and creeds serve us instead of us serving them.

In Jesus's gospel the people mattered. People hurt! People have social conflicts! People have psychological hang-ups! People live lives of quiet desperation! We must speak to these problems. Unless a doctrine or a tradition touches real life, real people, and real situations, it should be rejected or changed.

Religion has often been biased against science and technology. The weight of theology has been antiprogressive in medical and psychological disciplines. We seem to be afraid of intellectual truth. Why? If God created this cosmos, then all the truths it contains are his truths. The earth isn't flat, as religion once claimed. The sun doesn't go around the earth, as religion once claimed. Demons don't cause disease, as religion once claimed. Why can't we be mature agents of God and face reality?

To meet this challenge we must realize that Jesus gave us a mandate to discover and investigate when he declared, "Nothing shall be impossible to you." Now, Jesus didn't mean any one particular individual would be invincible. It's obvious that none of us is sufficient and perfect and able to effect all the necessary changes we need. He meant humankind in the universal sense is capable and indeed invincible! As we become autonomous, as we cooperate with each other, as we share knowledge, as we pool research data, and as we allow the Holy Spirit to reveal insights, we will be able to conquer evil, and "nothing shall be impossible" to us.

It's dangerous to allow strong religious convictions to override instincts, facts, and common sense. If you can't proudly and publicly proclaim a doctrine, then distrust it. As modern Christians we find it embarrassing and uncomfortable to say that Gandhi, Schweitzer, and Jefferson might be in an everlasting hell. Such obviously productive lives exemplify the very precepts Jesus stressed. Yet some fundamentalist doctrines seem to teach that unless they have had an exact "orthodox conversion," such people are condemned!

Since this belief appears ludicrous in light of a humane and sensible civilization, we must reexamine its assumptions. Our basic human feeling of the innate rightness of a principle is a God-given instinct. We should let common sense evaluate and guide our belief system. Written commandments of God won't contradict the urgings of the Holy Spirit, which are also of God.

False religion can cripple our intellect. Constantly having to twist reality in order to make it fit our personal creeds destroys our capacity to reason. Those who refuse to see, hear, and face facts will ultimately lose the ability to recognize facts, and that's fatal! A brainwashed mind can't distinguish delusion from reality. It can't discern propaganda from truth.

When you lose your ability to discriminate, you are at the mercy of every ideological wind that blows. Don't be dishonest with yourself. Don't rationalize and justify indefensible beliefs and practices. Trust your God-given resources of instinct and reason.

Finally, Christianity is not necessarily comforting and soothing. It can be in our darkest hours, but it can also be disturbing and disconcerting in our laziest moments. Jesus was not crucified because he said, "My peace I leave unto you," but rather because he said, "You generation of vipers." We don't have to swallow a set of unbelievable teachings to be accepted by God. We just have to take one step of faith and back it up with total commitment. So don't base your belief system on sensational tangents. Don't paint yourself into religious corners.

The kingdom is coming! Jesus's prayer for the kingdom to come on earth as it is in heaven will be answered. The ideal will be realized! The theoretical will become tangible! God's purposes will be accomplished!

The catch is this: The only hands, feet, minds, and voices God utilizes in this endeavor are ours! That's why we must project the direction of the church into the future. This may disturb some people who worship the status quo. Many members want to envision the church as absolutely unchangeable—the one constant in an out-of-control world.

Traditionalists express this philosophy in various illustrations: A man once dreamed of a city where there were many different buildings. There were stores, blacksmith shops, and log homes. In the midst of these buildings stood one plain, unpretentious structure. Men and women were going in and coming out.

In his dream a hundred years passed, and he found himself again in this same city. He hardly recognized it. All the former buildings had disappeared, and more imposing structures had taken their places. Still, in the midst of these buildings stood the same little modest structure with men and women going in and coming out.

In his dream a thousand years passed, and he returned to the same city. It was completely transformed. All the buildings he had seen before were gone, and new buildings with unbelievable architecture and great grandeur had taken their places, except right in the middle was that same simple little structure.

The man asked, "What is this institution that remains forever unchanged when everything else has been modernized?"

The answer came: "Oh! This is the house of God, the bastion of the old-time religion!"

What a naive attitude. Our knowledge constantly increases, our innovations constantly improve, and our experiences constantly add to our understanding of life. Why shouldn't the church reflect these advances? We don't consider it a virtue to farm exactly like people did in the first century. We don't want to work like they did or eat or dress or wash clothes like they did. Why, then, do we insinuate that the church must think and minister in precisely the same way the New

Testament disciples did? Haven't we learned anything is two thousand years?

Discoveries in the natural realm and inventions in the technological realm will affect and improve our theological beliefs. Why is it that our architecture can change, our communication can change, our lighting and heating systems can change, but our theological thinking must remain forever the same?

This is nonsense! Such outmoded ideas have prompted many to ask, "Do we still need the church?" It's an honest question, and different people have found their own answers. One woman said, "I don't go to any church or religious meetings now. My religion is being with God. I don't need any help with that."

A middle-aged Protestant clergyman expressed his dilemma: "I don't know what I believe about church doctrine. The main thing is that I have to support a wife, a kid in high school, and a girl in college. So I have to stand up on Sunday mornings and preach a sermon that won't get too many people mad. I have to go on being the 'man of God' even though I don't have any clear idea what that means anymore."

A Yale University student put it this way: "The church didn't lead in moral opposition to wars or racial injustice. In fact, it follows so far behind that you can scarcely see it. So the church is beyond hypocrisy for me. It's dull, irrelevant, and afraid of life. God is very much alive, but God doesn't need this church."

In fact, our worship often condones and supports our present lifestyle instead of analyzing its integrity and encouraging its growth.

A manufactured theology unconnected to a moral center is destructive. Americans are looking for pragmatic answers as they struggle to make spiritual sense out of their lives. They are worried about drugs and crime, war atrocities and racial inequality, high taxes and overcrowded schools, ecological crises and politics. They are also worried about machines that break down and prices that go up, lack of security in old age and personal anguish in the face of a collapse of values. Most people today aren't interested in first-century or nineteenth-century answers to questions about faith. They don't care what an ancient church council thought or decreed. They want answers that have meaning for their own lives now!

The institutional church must quit talking to itself and recognize the honesty of the many dropouts and the validity of their questions. Hordes of people have repudiated old voices of authority that speak from "on high" concerning matters about which they know nothing. This sharp reaction against institutional religion holds both promise and danger. In the future the church may take forms that we cannot presently imagine.

The church is not simply a building on the corner. The church is greater and more inclusive than most of us believe, yet it's an intimate community. Jesus promised he would be present "wherever two or three are gathered together." The church links us to a healing ministry of love.

Jeremiah sensed the future of the church when he quoted the Lord, saying,

> I will make a new covenant with the house of Israel and the house of Judah. It will not be like the covenant that I made with their ancestors when I took them by the hand to bring them out of the land of Egypt—a covenant that they broke, though I was their husband, says the LORD. But this is the covenant that I will make with the house of Israel after those days, says the LORD: I will put my law within them, and I will write it on their hearts, and I will be their God, and they shall be my people. No longer shall they teach one another or say to each other, "Know the LORD," for they shall all know me, from the least of them to the greatest, says the LORD, for I will forgive their iniquity and remember their sin no more. (Jer 31:31–34)

John, in Revelation, echoed this same sentiment, saying, "I saw no temple in the city, for its temple is the Lord God the Almighty and the Lamb. And the city has no need of sun or moon to shine on it, for the glory of God is its light, and its lamp is the Lamb. The nations will walk by its light" (Rev 21:22–24).

In other words, the church should be trying desperately to "work itself out of a job." It must do this by permeating all of life. Its values must shape the economic policies and political processes. Its principles must set individuals free to be autonomous, productive agents. This is happening!

Educational institutions, welfare offices, foreign aid programs, labor laws, and all humane organizations are evidence of the kingdom working. Artificial rituals and irrelevant dogmas will become less important in a scientifically oriented world, but loving God and our neighbors will never become obsolete.

The church in this sense is invincible.

One astute pastor quit preaching and expressed this opinion:

> "Over the years I've notice three types of people: First, the church exists because of a few people. These dedicated members comprise about ten percent of the congregation, but they do about ninety percent of the work. Without them congregations couldn't survive.
>
> Second, the church exists in spite of some people. An old preacher described them when he was asked how many active members his church had. He replied, "Oh, they're all active. About half are for the Lord, and the other half are for the devil!"
>
> Third, the church exists for the benefit of multitudes of people; especially for the last, the least, and the lost. It exists for the lonely, the troubled, the needy, the rejected and everyone else who seeks fellowship with God.

So does the church exist because of you? In spite of you? For you?

If we are part of the "because" group, we can be certain that our outreach and influence will endure to Mars and beyond, even to the twenty-fifth century. We can be sure that our church is truly "marching to Zion" rather than "stumbling to Zion."

Paul said, "Christ loved the church and gave himself up for her" (Eph 5:25).

Jesus said, "On this rock I will build my church, and the gates of Hades will not prevail against it" (Matt 16:18).